This book is a gift. It's gorgeously honest, offering the reader both solidarity and rapport. It's hopeful, in the most down-to-earth, truthful sense. And it's an inspiring call to meet God in the midst of the sorrow we all eventually become acquainted with. Having my own grief experience, I found Eric to be a true brother, a fellow traveler, and one who offers a rich variety of truth to feed on. You won't find empty platitudes here. Please read. Enter the search for God in suffering, the beauty of pain, and the offer of strength.

KATE MERRICK, author of *And Still She Laughs* and *Here, Now*

Because I was in their wedding, I was a witness to the first things of Eric and Elizabeth's life together. Over these past years, I have witnessed the terrible beauty of a couple that is now, too soon, facing the last things together. They have borne this calamity with courage, fidelity, and honor. How have they done that? It is not through comforting themselves with trite answers or finding techniques for making the horrors of our cursed world somehow less awful. What they have done is humbly rely on God's grace to sustain them, always reflecting on the truths taught by Christians for millennia, the truths that Eric writes about so beautifully in this book. Reading this will help you learn to love the God that Eric and Elizabeth love, the God who is their (and our) comfort, even in the deepest darkness.

JAKE MEADOR, editor-in-chief of Mere Orthodoxy

In his refreshingly honest book, Eric Tonjes shows us what it means to preach the gospel to ourselves in suffering and grief. I appreciate his candor because it will encourage the body of Christ to run straight to Jesus in their pain, not away from him. I'm happy to recommend this beautiful book to those who are hurting since a vision of our glorious, always-present God and our eternal future with him is what we most need.

KRISTEN WETHERELL, author of *F
coauthor of *Hope When It Hurts*

D1056880

I don't believe I've ever come across something quite like this: the sophistication of a pastor-theologian who obviously knows a great deal about the nature of God combined with an individual who is personally gutted with grief. In these tender, wisdom-soaked pages, follow Eric Tonjes, who has gone to the depths of human anguish and lived to tell the honest story of how he and his wife were met by the God who suffers with us and who ushers us into a deeper intimacy with life itself. Eric is the kind of pastor everybody wants at their side when facing inexplicable pain.

REV. DR. ERIC E. PETERSON,
pastor of Colbert Presbyterian Church, author of *Letters to a Young Congregation* and (with Eugene H. Peterson) *Letters to a Young Pastor*

Numerous forces at work in modern Western culture shape us to be people who avoid the waves of grief for fear of being overwhelmed. Many Christians in this context attempt to keep God at a distance as well, as if even God might be overtaken by the helplessness of loss. Eric Tonjes shows us a different path. In his poignant and direct way, Tonjes welcomes us on an experiential and theological pilgrimage: Amid our gasping in the waves of loss, the Lord of creation enables us to breathe, to both wrestle with and rest in him. In a book about loss and hope, mortality and divine glory, Tonjes bears witness to human and divine mysteries we so often suppress or ignore.

J. TODD BILLINGS,
author of *Rejoicing in Lament* and *The End of the Christian Life*

This is a book Eric Tonjes never wanted to be qualified to write, but one the rest of us urgently need to read. Grief comes calling on us all, and we have no choice but to open the doors of our hearts to the agony of eventually losing someone we love. In *Either Way, We'll Be All Right*, Tonjes takes us with him as he experiences the searing pain of seeing his wife eaten alive by cancer. In brutally beautiful prose yet without self-pity, he eloquently wraps language around deep sorrow while pointing the way to a loving God who meets us in our grief.

MAGGIE WALLEM ROWE, speaker, dramatist, and author of *This Life We Share*

Here, written by one who is suffering, is a book that will serve the suffering. And in a fallen world, all of us will tomorrow find ourselves in that category, even if we are not shedding tears today. Reflecting on his own journey, Eric Tonjes explains with the heart of a pastor how the tears of grief are a lens through which we can most clearly see the beauty and glory of Christ such that we recognize, in Eric's words, that "our vision of God on the throne provides a resource like no other for moving forward under the weight of grief." Eric's thoughts are not just the raw journal entries of a man whose wife has cancer. Rather, his reflections are built on a foundation of rock-solid theology. This is a book that will serve both our minds and our emotions. I highly recommend it.

CHRIS BRAUNS, D. MIN, pastor of The Red Brick Church, author of *Unpacking Forgiveness*

It is tempting to say that what qualifies someone to speak meaningfully about suffering is their experience of suffering. But I don't think that's right. For the believer, what qualifies us to speak meaningfully about suffering is our knowledge of God in the midst of it. Eric Tonjes does this brilliantly. No whitewashing, no side-stepping, no false hope. Just the gospel of God-with-us, God-for-us, forever.

ANDREW ARNDT, lead pastor of New Life East, author of *All Flame*

I waded into Eric Tonjes's manuscript with honest dread—another account of the sad journey of a loving couple into cancer's darkness. I have read it before, lived it before, wept through it before, and did not welcome the weight of it again. And then I began to read. Contrary to my expectations, I found joyful love, honest—really honest—grief, sweet family bonds, humor so out of place that it helps, profound faith, hope to share, and remarkably compelling writing. The long day's journey into night never materialized. Instead, I found myself cheering these champions of the race that will be lost—and then won.

BRYAN CHAPELL, pastor and author

By the time this book is published, our music pastor will have died. His family has watched him diminish in front of their eyes as cancer overtakes him. He watches it himself and mourns. It is one of the most impossible of situations imaginable. Fears and questions abound. This book sits in their home as a companion for their unplanned journey in uncharted territory. Who understands this path better but one who is on it as well? Eric Tonjes offers himself as a fellow pilgrim, traveling on a road none wish to take. He wrestles openly and unapologetically both with the fears and questions entwined with death and with the God who is sovereign over all. His message to you: *Take heart; you do not walk this path alone.*

SARAH VAN DIEST, author of *God in the Dark*

EITHER WAY, WE'LL BE ALL RIGHT

AN HONEST EXPLORATION OF GOD IN OUR GRIEF

ERIC TONJES

A NavPress resource published in alliance
with Tyndale House Publishers

NavPress is the publishing ministry of The Navigators, an international Christian organization and leader in personal spiritual development. NavPress is committed to helping people grow spiritually and enjoy lives of meaning and hope through personal and group resources that are biblically rooted, culturally relevant, and highly practical.

For more information, visit NavPress.com.

Either Way, We'll Be All Right: An Honest Exploration of God in Our Grief

Copyright © 2021 by Eric Tonjes. All rights reserved.

A NavPress resource published in alliance with Tyndale House Publishers

NAVPRESS and the NavPress logo are registered trademarks of NavPress, The Navigators, Colorado Springs, CO. *TYNDALE* is a registered trademark of Tyndale House Ministries. Absence of ® in connection with marks of NavPress or other parties does not indicate an absence of registration of those marks.

The Team:
Caitlyn Carlson, Acquisitions Editor; Elizabeth Schroll, Copy Editor; Olivia Eldredge, Operations Manager; Nicole Grimes, Designer

Cover photograph of waves by Omar Roque on Unsplash. All rights reserved.

Author photo taken by Emilynne Photography, copyright © 2020. All rights reserved.

Published in association with the literary agent Don Gates of The Gates Group, www.the-gates-group.com.

Unless otherwise indicated, all Scripture quotations are from The ESV® Bible (The Holy Bible, English Standard Version®), copyright © 2001 by Crossway, a publishing ministry of Good News Publishers. Used by permission. All rights reserved.

Some of the anecdotal illustrations in this book are true to life and are included with the permission of the persons involved. All other illustrations are composites of real situations, and any resemblance to people living or dead is purely coincidental.

For information about special discounts for bulk purchases, please contact Tyndale House Publishers at csresponse@tyndale.com, or call 1-855-277-9400.

ISBN 978-1-64158-320-6

Printed in the United States of America

27	26	25	24	23	22	21
7	6	5	4	3	2	1

For Elizabeth.
Even knowing the last pages,
I'd gladly write the story again.

CONTENTS

Introduction

I AM WATCHING my wife die of cancer.

That reality has defined the last few years of our lives. There are moments where it has a strange, stark beauty. We have learned something like wisdom from the pain. It has kindled a deep affection we never would have tasted without teetering on the brink of her mortality. She has shown a grace and peace in her suffering that has displayed Jesus to me and to many others.

Cancer's reality has also been brutal, leaving in my soul churning pools of existential despair and spiritual rage.

As a pastor, I don't think I'm supposed to admit that last bit. People are willing to accept an "It's hard," a long-suffering grimace and blithe platitude. They get uncomfortable when you admit the horror of suffering. It doesn't fit with their picture of spirituality as something upbeat and encouraging. Yet anything less than the ugly truth is an injustice to the reality of a wife and mother in her mid-thirties being eaten alive by warped parts of her own body.

At the same time, as a Christian, I mean the first part too. Amid cancer's agony and wrongness, I have found graces that tear praises from my pressed lips. God has shown up for us, not in some sanctimonious way, but for real. I have yelled at him and wrestled with him and found his arms around me still, hugging me until the turmoil subsides. He has been a Father to us both, and a fellow sufferer, an adversary, and a lover.

I write this book out of the collision of those realities. We are in the middle of the pain and the provision. I am not reflecting on some tragedy long past, observing with the tranquilizing distance of time. These words are immediate and soaked with tears. In part, I'm writing to try to make sense of the agony and hope that both grip my heart. I'm also hoping that, if you are on a similar road, you might find something familiar that helps you survive.

Here is what this book is not:

- This book is not a solution for the pain you are feeling. There is nothing that can make life's wrongness okay.
- This book is not a book about asking for and receiving miracles from God. He can provide healing, but he also sanctifies suffering.
- This book is not about practical strategies to cope with sorrow, although we'll talk a bit about some practices that are helpful.
- This book is not about holding myself up as an example. If there are lessons here, they have been learned through my own sins and mistakes.

I write this book out of two convictions. One is that all of us, especially those of us in pain, need honesty. I find something soul nourishing in encountering a pilgrim on Christ's road who is willing to show their callouses and scars. In these pages, I will do my best to reveal mine.

The second is that, even more than such authenticity, we need an experience of God. Every human problem is ultimately theological, not in the sense that we can find an explanation in thick books with Latin phrases but in that our response flows from how we think about God. What we need in our grief is to encounter him. He meets us in our heartbreak and carries us toward healing, although healing is not the same as being whole.

We cannot "solve" sorrow, especially in its first staggering waves. At the beginning of grief, there is nothing someone can do but feel it. And nothing in these pages will change that. Grief, after all, is a process. Just because you and I might both be experiencing it doesn't mean we are side by side. I can only speak out of my experience, and maybe yours is different. That's fine.

But there comes a point where we must move forward and maybe even look for answers. Some of what I write is aimed at those in that latter place. If that isn't you yet, I understand. Read or don't read, as much as you feel is helpful. Give yourself the freedom to simply feel what you need to feel.

In the later stages of grief, while the initial all-consuming shock has passed, it can still be painful to confront what we feel head-on. One of the most difficult things for me has been realizing that sometimes we need to be challenged, even when we are in the shadowy valley. Tumors must be cut out before healing can come, but my heart aches, knowing how painful that can be. It is destructive to lock our grief away in a closet, but we will also be destroyed if we let it rush in all at once. Walk slowly, leaning on Jesus.

A few words about where we're going. This book is divided into several sections. The first two chapters will address some general ideas about God and the world that set the stage for our journey. The next eight chapters, divided into pairs, will then invite us to explore from several angles how God meets us in our grief. The final three chapters offer some practical discussions about walking through sorrow and then sum up the vision of God we need.

My prayers, as frail and stammered as they sometimes are, are with you. I hope you find some comfort here, and some truth, and the strength to walk forward in the valley of the shadow of death. In this season, I have frequently returned to an old collection of Puritan prayers. Its first supplication reminds us that "the valley is the place of vision." And so we pray,

> *Let me find thy light in my darkness,*
> *thy life in my death,*
> *thy joy in my sorrow,*
> *thy grace in my sin,*
> *thy riches in my poverty,*
> *thy glory in my valley.*[1]

This is what I have found and what I hope you do as well. Our tears, when we gaze through them, can transform from a veil for our eyes to a lens that brings into sharper focus the deep things of God. And as we so behold him, he will meet us and carry us until the day he at last dries our weeping eyes.

PART I

The Journey of Grief

Talking about sorrow is like catching a jellyfish barehanded. It is rigid words grasping at amorphous reality, the fullness of it squirting through my fingers (as I get repeatedly stung in the process). Even if, with words, I manage to pin it to a few of these pages, the dried-out husk left behind fails to express the creature swimming in my gut.

There are various biblical images of grief. It is a sleepless groaning, a twisting of the stomach, a swollen tongue that chokes the mouth, and a drunken bender of the heart. It pierces us with arrows. It dissolves our bones, leaving us slumping bags of flesh. As I seek to wrap language around sorrow in these pages, understand that no one is more aware than I of the limitations of such an endeavor. To truly name a thing is to comprehend it, to have a sort of power over it. Grief is the ultimate powerlessness. The man who pretends to control it will be quickly proved a liar.

Yet though I cannot truly name the thing, I hope to gesture in its direction. What we are discussing is a journey. I cannot capture every painful vista in these pages. I certainly cannot give shortcuts or clear directions. What I can do is describe the landmarks of sorrow, the vistas and valleys I have experienced along the way. Perhaps, as a fellow traveler, some of it will look familiar—and together, we can learn that we are not alone.

1

CONFRONTING SUFFERING

GOD FIRST KICKED US IN THE TEETH seven years ago. I was finishing seminary. My wife, Elizabeth, and I were expecting our first child. We went to the OB-GYN for a routine visit. Moments after entering the room, the doctor hurried out with a worried look. He returned a few minutes later and told us that Elizabeth was about to give birth. We needed to get to a hospital as soon as possible.

She was twenty-seven weeks pregnant, on the cusp of her third trimester.

A numbness took hold as those words seeped into my brain. Careening along the shoulder of the highway past rush-hour traffic, I felt detached. I was an observer, sitting outside my body. We staggered into the emergency room. I gave a matter-of-fact explanation to the tired nurse behind the glass. Unable to halt the labor, they transferred her to another hospital. I followed the ambulance, still in a daze.

I remember our daughter's birth in vivid moments. Doctors arguing with surgeons. Hymns I softly sang. Her scream as she was born, tiny and gray. My joyful sob because that feeble cry meant our daughter's lungs were at least developed enough to hold air.

Then the numbness returned.

For the first time in my life, I was confronted by mortality and the terror and sorrow that accompanies it. We didn't know if our daughter would survive. Her beating heart was visible through gossamer skin. Some moments as she lay in the NICU, it paused, forgetting to pump, and we would shake and cajole her back to life. We watched her, in a sense, die and be reborn again and again.

In seminary, they make you give practice sermons to fellow students. Like most young men studying for ministry, I was far too confident of my prowess. I had chosen, a week before our daughter's birth, to preach on Abraham's sacrifice of Isaac. It seemed poignant and courageous when my wife was five months pregnant. Now, realizing that God may well be asking us to surrender our child in a literal sense, the story left me gutted. I felt the horror of those words: "Abraham reached out his hand and took the knife to slaughter his son" (Genesis 22:10). Seeing my daughter laid out in her incubator, tangled in wires, I knew the fear and trembling that must have seized the patriarch.

Numbness became my shelter as I confronted the specter of death. My emotions seemed too big, too incomprehensible to confront, so I shut down. I locked my heart behind steel blast doors, unassailable and unfeeling. In one way, it worked. The numbness helped me survive. It was only later, over the months we lived at the hospital, that I began to recognize it came with a cost.

C. S. Lewis comments—in *The Four Loves*—on the dilemma I faced: "To love at all is to be vulnerable. Love anything, and your heart will certainly be wrung and possibly be broken. If you want to make sure of keeping it intact, you must give your heart to no one. . . . Lock it up safe in the casket or coffin of your selfishness. But in that casket—safe, dark, motionless, airless—it will change. It will not be broken; it will become unbreakable, impenetrable, irredeemable."[1]

About two months after our daughter's birth, I had a moment of clarity. Holding her fingers, stroking her hair, I realized I felt nothing. My hands were performing the actions of a loving parent, but my heart was a sealed room. What started as a tool for survival was beginning to turn me distant and cold. Unless the sorrow and fear I felt were confronted, I knew I would forever be a mere facsimile of a father to our girl.

That recognition didn't instantly change my heart. I was just holding on from day to day. It took months of counseling and years of reflection to name what I unconsciously realized in that moment. There was something wrong with how my heart responded to suffering. Something planted deep in my soul by the culture I had grown up in kept me from appropriately entering into grief.

Our Culture's Silence

Our world doesn't know what to do with sorrow and death. While nobody likes these painful realities, they pose a special problem to our way of thinking. Our sophisticated Western civilization is rendered speechless before the grave.

I've seen it firsthand as we've confronted my wife's terminal diagnosis. There's that word, *terminal*. It, like *incurable* and other euphemisms, has an appropriate sense of finality but avoids the awfulness of the truth. When I get tired of doublespeak, I sometimes start using the *D* word in those conversations. "My wife is dying." "After she dies." I can see people flinch when I say it. We cannot handle naked statements of mortality.

Part of this discomfort is simply that death is invisible to many of us. Sure, we see it on the television, but there it is mediated to us by the smooth, perpetually youthful faces of actors and newscasters. In our personal lives, it is almost entirely absent. We put the sick in hospitals. We ensconce the elderly in nursing homes. Many people I know have never seen a corpse, at least not before the alchemy of embalming restores its lifelike luster.

That isn't how it used to be; for most of history, doctors came to houses and disease was on semipublic display. As infant mortality has plummeted and life expectancy has stretched and technology has made us safer, consciousness of our fragility has drained away.

Of course, these advances have great benefits. Our premature daughter would have been dead in minutes if she had been born twenty years earlier. But somewhere along the way, we crossed a threshold. Disease and dying became too alien, so we hid them away.

In the past, grief was a public process. The bereaved would wear black clothes and veil their faces. They would weep in the streets. Torn shirts, sackcloths, and ashes on their foreheads were intentionally visible marks of sorrow. We have banished such public grieving. When we encounter it today, which is rare, we seem to think the person must have a disorder. *It can't be healthy to wear pain so openly*, we think, judging those people for a lack of self-restraint. As a result, sorrow ends up hidden. It festers in our hearts, but we suppose we must be abnormal in how we experience it because we do not see it in others.

Our efforts to hide grief and death from view, though, are not the root issue. We shut our eyes because our way of viewing the world can't handle people dying. It exposes the lies we believe.

For most of history, people received meaning in their lives from something outside themselves. Maybe it was in serving family and community. Maybe it was in the invisible currency of "honor." Maybe it was in serving a higher power. Each of these approaches came with issues, but they could all handle mortality. Family and community would continue after someone was gone. Dying an honorable death was the goal of an honorable life. The gods live on, and perhaps in death, a person lived on with them.

But in our world today, things are different. We get meaning from within ourselves. We're chasing self-realization and self-fulfillment, becoming our best selves and living the American dream. There are good things about this individualism, but it starts to unravel when it faces the grave. Death is the final self-dissolution. It is the end of the pursuit of happiness. Our culture offers no comfort in death, just a fatalistic acknowledgment that even the best party ends someday. "Have fun while it lasts," we are told, "and try not to notice the ticking of the clock and the aging face in the mirror."

Our form of Christianity is equally unhelpful. We have reimagined our religion to fit the world we inhabit, starting with the things it values and then making Jesus meet those desires. Sometimes this is obvious. Our culture tells us the goal of existence is finding yourself and being comfortable; we make Jesus into the ultimate guru of self-esteem. The culture desires material possessions; Jesus' promised blessings turn into Porsches and McMansions, and all that biblical stuff about the perils of wealth doesn't really mean what it says. The world wants to sin without repercussions; Jesus is all about being welcoming and never judging.

However, the compromise can also sneak in at the edges. One of the good things the church seeks to do is answer the questions of the surrounding culture. It seeks to be relevant, to contextualize Christ's message in a way that people will understand. That goal is noble, but it comes with a hidden cost. If we only respond to the world's inquiries, we lose significant parts of the Christian message. Jesus stands to the world as a question before he offers it any answers. He is a provocation, a mirror within which we recognize what is broken about our way of thinking and living. The cross wasn't Rome's response to a failure to adequately contextualize but an attempt to kill the question Jesus posed.

Because our culture cannot bear to look at death, and because the church has sought to meet the culture on its own terms, we often fail to speak of dying. Aphorisms ("They're in a better place") are aimed at ending discussions, not beginning them. "Heaven is real," we say, as if what that means is, "Don't worry about the fact that in a few short years, your body will break down, worms will eat your flesh, and you will vanish from the earth and have to give an account to your Creator."

Of course, it hasn't always been this way. In fact, the reality of death and dying used to be ever-present in Christian literature and poetry. A bestselling genre of books for centuries was *ars moriendi*, the "art of dying." Old hymns are full of refrains about suffering, pain, and mortality. Past saints lived in eras when death could not be hidden, so they confronted it. We do not.

Christians, just like the broader world, try to hide life's dark corners. You can feel it in the ways we often try to give comfort. "It will be okay," we might say, and while in a sense that is ultimately true, it is also definably false. There is nothing "okay" about children losing their mother or the world losing the unique blessing of a human life. "We're here for you, whatever you need." The help is welcome, but what we really need, a cure for cancer and the deeper disease of mortality, isn't on offer, and a frozen casserole can't take that away. What we almost never say is what should be our starting place: "Death is terrible. I am sorry. This is not how it should be."

I understand that it is hard to know what to say. I've learned to regard such responses with sympathy and even appreciation for the heart they show. What they reveal, though, is a discomfort with the reality of the world. Death and anguish, disease and mourning are all guaranteed parts of the human condition. Christians, more than anyone, should be able to acknowledge them directly.

Learning Lament

Smack dab in the middle of the Bible is the book of Psalms, a collection of poems that formed the hymnbook for ancient Israel. These were the songs they sang together in worship, the lyrics that were furrowed into their memories. The book of Psalms is not uncomfortable with grief or hardship or death; it is its constant refrain.

Just start flipping through the Psalms: "O LORD, how many are my foes! Many are rising against me" (Psalm 3:1); "Give ear to my words, O LORD; consider my groaning" (Psalm 5:1); "Be gracious to me, O LORD, for I am languishing; heal me, O LORD, for my bones are troubled. My soul also is greatly troubled. But you, O LORD—how long?" (Psalm 6:2-3); "Why, O LORD, do you stand far away? Why do you hide yourself in times of trouble?" (Psalm 10:1). Of the first ten psalms, seven are cries of heartache or repentance in the face of suffering, and there are 140 to go.

As an extreme example, read Psalm 88. Go ahead, you can pause and read through it. Try doing it out loud; taste the words. The Sons of Korah, who wrote it, start with a cry to the Lord and then recount a life full of struggle. They feel like they are teetering on the brink of death (Psalm 88:3-6). They are drowning under an ocean of grief (Psalm 88:7, 16-17). Their friends have abandoned them, and God himself seems to have turned his back (Psalm 88:8-12). The psalm wallows in anguish—and at the end, they are still in that terrible place. No happy ending tied up in a bow; rather, "You have caused my beloved and my friend to shun me; my companions have become darkness" (Psalm 88:18).

Few of the Psalms sit only in the darkness, but many pass through it. Consider Psalm 22, which Jesus himself quoted from the cross. It starts with the most gut-wrenching cry: "My God, my God, why have you forsaken me?" (Psalm 22:1). What follows is a picture of a person wrestling with God and with his own heart. The psalmist names something true: "Yet you are holy, enthroned on the praises of Israel" (Psalm 22:3). Then he collapses back into the reality of life: "I am a worm and not a man, scorned by mankind and despised by the people" (Psalm 22:6). Another note of hope: "Yet you are he who took me from the womb; you made me trust you at my mother's breasts" (Psalm 22:9). Another tormented cry: "I am poured out like water, and all my bones are out of joint; my heart is like wax; it is melted within my breast" (Psalm 22:14). This is, consistently, the pattern of these "psalms of lament." They call us to find hope in the Lord, but they do it while also acknowledging our broken hearts and circumstances.

These divinely inspired songs stand as a rebuke to our discomfort with grief. The Bible doesn't shrink from pain; it names our sorrows and brings them before the throne of God. Even more shockingly, it invites us to sing of them to God and together as God's people. Just imagine what it would communicate if we stood with our brothers and sisters in worship and sang, "Why have you forsaken me? I am a worm and not a human being."

A dear friend who has struggled with depression tells me what comfort he finds in these psalms. He feels like, in our world, the darkness in his heart is something he must disguise. Others would judge him or try to fix him if he shared it. The way we handle depression is symptomatic of our broader failure to confront the darkness. This is especially true for Christians who treat it as something to be dismissed: "Snap out of it. Get over yourself. Just cheer up and trust in Jesus!" As if it were so simple. Our failure can also be manifested in more therapeutic solutions. As much as counseling and medication can be sweet balms for those trapped in the cycles of clinical depression, at times, they become excuses to fix rather than reasons to feel. Sorrow becomes like a variant strain of influenza. Neither those in denial nor those rushing to remedies are willing to confront the deeper truth that life can bring great sadness and that we ought to feel it.

Of course, the Psalms don't leave us with only despair. Most of them also come with an invitation to move toward God. Psalm 22 does arrive at a place of hoping for divine deliverance. It calls those who fear God to praise his name and ends with a heart-lifting picture of God's Kingdom covering the earth and gathering the nations. Even Psalm 88 brings its darkness before the Lord, repeatedly seeking his presence.

Yet this pattern does not mean that the psalmist's struggle is over. Instead, this movement of grief to praise is meant to be repeated over and over. The Psalms are not transcriptions of a counseling session or a self-help talk, offering a method to solve our problems; they are the daily cries of God's people. They are a hymnbook. Over and over, week after week, those singing them would confront the darkness and remind themselves of their hope.

Entering Grief

Which brings us back to my stony heart as I stood beside my daughter's hospital bed. I was doing everything in my power to stay aloof from grief, keeping it safely contained and out of sight. What I had missed—what the Christian culture I had grown up in had failed to teach me—was that, while there is hope in Jesus, we can only experience that hope by entering the darkness.

As a pastor, I sometimes counsel people with significant wounds from their past. Their tendency is to "stuff it," to lock away the hurt in some hidden corner of their brains. This response is normal. When they first experience those traumas, it is even necessary. If any of us bore the weight of all the sadness in our lives at once, we would be crushed.

The issue with this approach is that it can change over time from a survival mechanism to a habit. We stuff everything into that compartment, deny it is there, and throw away the key. Yet grief will not be ignored. Pressure builds against the walls we erect. Cracks start to form. The only way to keep it in is to make ourselves harder and harder. Any emotion becomes a risk, any attachment a potential chink in our armor, so in the name of avoiding sorrow, we end up losing joy and love—and finally, the capacity for any feeling at all.

We must realize, when we talk about beginning to lower that barrier, that things will get worse before they get better. The only way to relieve the pressure is to face some of the pain. This was certainly true of my own experiences. The way I handled my daughter's near death was the culmination of years of compartmentalization. As I started to confront what I was feeling, it wrecked me. I was plunged into the waters of despair. It was miserable.

On the other side, though, lay something that was worth it. By walking into those wounds, I became able to break through numbness and feel my love for our little girl. Even more, it gave me the tools to be present amid the further grief Elizabeth's cancer has brought.

In John Bunyan's *Pilgrim's Progress*, the Pilgrim (Christian), brought at last to the end of the expedition, confronts the waters of death alongside his companion Hopeful. Before them is the Celestial City, the object of their quest, but between them and its gates is a deep river with no bridge. Their companions tell them that they cannot reach the city except by passing through its churning depths. They don't have to make this final journey. They can turn back and live a while longer. Yet what Christian and Hopeful both recognize is that only by passing through the waters can they reach the joy of the far shore.

For Bunyan, the river is an image of physical death. Yet it speaks also to the many smaller deaths we confront every day. Christian's dilemma teaches us a crucial principle: The way to life always lies through death. The way to healing always passes through pain. We must step into the Jordan before we can reach the far shore.

Our modern world teaches us to avoid sorrow, to drown it out with distraction or self-medication or positivity. Modern Christianity seeks to use Jesus for this same end, as a way to stay positive and be encouraged and never confront the river that looms. These approaches can help us keep it together temporarily, but they can never offer us life. Only by plunging into the waters, half-sure we will drown, can we reach the city of light.

Here is the question I have been confronting these last years as I have faced my wife's impending death: Is this a river I will seek to cross, or will I hide here on the shore? I am writing this book in an attempt to walk into the water, to name the sorrow in my heart and wade deeper into the Jordan's currents.

How do we make such a painful journey? In the middle of the river, Pilgrim is overwhelmed by doubt and despair. He is convinced that he will drown. Hopeful, though, finds sure footing and helps his friend. What makes the difference is that Hopeful is sustained by a set of truths deep in his heart—truths of Scripture that he cries to his sinking friend—and by a vision of their destination. "Brother," he says, "I see the gate and men standing by it to receive us."[2] If we fix our eyes on the hope of life on the far shore and walk forward with God's promises in our hearts, the water ceases to be a barrier and becomes instead the road to life.

Christianity does not remove our suffering. It calls us to plunge into sorrow up to our necks. The good news is that it also offers us a vision of the world and of God that provide the resources we need to survive.

2

BEAUTIFUL AND BROKEN

ONE OF THE DELIGHTS of marriage is relishing the physicality of the beloved. Marital love is more than physical intimacy, but that doesn't mean it is less. It involves a delight in the body, a wondering at the particular beauty of this particular body. Romantic love in Scripture is carnal as well as spiritual (Proverbs 5:18-19; Song of Songs 4:1-8). While there are many other components of a godly marriage, we ought not lose the God-given goodness of things as basic as sex and touch and closeness. This is true of our marriage—I delight in my beloved and she (for reasons I don't understand) seems to delight in me.

Part of what makes cancer so bizarre is the way it hides in

the shadow of our own bodies. It is not an outside intruder like a stabbing blade or virus. Instead, something within my bride has become twisted. The physicality in which I delight is the thing slowly killing her. The realization of this rears up when I least expect it. I see her standing in the doorway, a summer dress catching her curves, and this awful knowledge superimposes itself. Right now, in her gut, there are twisted parts of her stretching out tendrils to choke her from within.

Cancer makes it acute, but we all feel this tension. There is an ambiguity that accompanies our physicality. The body is a divine gift. It is the source of many of our deepest pleasures. Anyone who has eaten a well-prepared meal or tasted water with a parched mouth recognizes that there is something good about our flesh. The warmth of the sun, the tickle of a breeze, the brush of another's skin—all these speak deep happiness to our souls.

Yet the body is also the source of our deepest pains. Perhaps it isn't mutated tumors, but all of us feel its limitations and frailties. We can feel imprisoned in our own skin by disease or age or the way our bodies were abused. Physical delight walks hand in hand with the potential for physical destruction.

One of our struggles in my wife's diagnosis is owning both sides of this at once. If we ignored the cancer in her flesh, we would be choosing a lie that cannot last. We must believe it to endure the horrific treatments necessary to contain it. Yet to lose the glory of physicality will result in despair. I lie next to Elizabeth and rest my hand on her stomach and feel desire and the rough edges of scars from surgeries and joy at the children given life beneath that skin and revulsion at the tentacles of tumors in her abdomen that will eventually tear us apart.

This conflicted relationship with physicality isn't new; it has always been a part our story. From its first pages, Scripture gives us a picture of the world that is transcendently glorious and horribly disfigured.

Rightness and Wrongness

There is both a rightness and a wrongness to the world. I have been living with that contradiction wrapped around my heart. Daily life showers bright sparks. A child's laugh. A sideways glance from Elizabeth. A mirthful dinner table. Each of these blessings is like the rise of a roller coaster—at the top my stomach lurches, bracing for the inevitable fall. Where will the laughter be when my children are left without a mother? What will I do when I am left alone? How will we escape the looming reality of the chair that will soon be empty? Each joy is an open window providing ingress to the grief.

This world is both beautiful and broken. That is where we must start. It *is* outrageously beautiful. Just pick a flower from your garden and really look at it—the subtle striations of color in its petals, the splotches and patterns, the preposterous dimensions of a stamen, and the crystalline pollen on its tip. This flower is a fusion of art and artifice, of design and playfulness, and it demands wonder as it carpets meadows and bursts untended from the dirt.

It is worth stressing that wonder because there are those who miss it. For some, it is hidden by the curtain of despair. That's me, some days. For others in our age of economy and science, the world is mechanized and abstracted in a way that strips it of its poetry. Yet for all our blindness, creation still stands as a constant testimony of glory. I have seen thunderheads roll in over a prairie, the churning front roiling with rain and stuttering with lightning. I have watched a spider spin its web, strands disconcertingly stretching from its abdomen, and returned to see those same strands transformed into diamond jewelry by the dew. I have been present for the absurd marvel of childbirth. There is an artistry to the world that screams praise to heaven.

At the same time, this world is broken and disfigured. I have walked through the rubble of a town struck by a tornado and seen the dazed faces of those who lost their homes and history and identity in a single gust of wind. I have heard people say cruel things to my children and my children say things just as cruel. There are tubes pumping poison into my wife in the hopes it will kill the cancer faster than it kills her. There are moments when what my heart desires is to hurt and punish and destroy.

This world is both beautiful and broken, and we must insist that both are true. To lose our ability to see the beauty is to lose what makes us human; all that is left are the animal drives to eat and reproduce and survive. To lose our ability to see the brokenness makes us inhuman. True evil is never done with a grimace but with a smile and the best of intentions.

One of the things I love about Christianity is that it gives us names and reasons for both realities, weaving them together in how it explains the world.

All Very Good

In its opening pages, Scripture gives us words for our experiences. The Bible's story begins with God's creation of the universe. His work is pictured in the form of a workweek; God is the craftsman, much like an Israelite who would have practiced some trade, except what he makes is not a spearhead or clay jar but the whole shebang. Stars and mountains and pine trees and elephants, all the product of six days' labor. It is not even portrayed as especially difficult; God speaks and things spring into being. This story is meant to teach us several things. It shows God's absolute power over the earth, it reminds us that everything belongs to him, and it speaks of the character of creation itself.

God is a perfect craftsman, and so there is goodness in what he creates. The world's excellence is one of the core themes of Genesis 1. God separates the light from the darkness: "God said, 'Let there be light,' and there was light" (Genesis 1:3). Then, in the very next verse, he steps back, looks over what he has made, and announces his take: "God saw that the light was good" (Genesis 1:4). This isn't just an incidental aside. God speaks this piece of creation into being, and then he also speaks to us of how we should feel about it. If we fail to recognize the goodness in creation, we are disagreeing with its Maker.

This pattern is repeated for each step in the process. God speaks, then declares, "Good. Good. Good." Finally, after forming humanity as this world's caretakers, God reaffirms and heightens his judgment: "God saw everything that he had made, and behold, it was *very good*" (Genesis 1:31, emphasis added).

The plot is about to twist, of course, and we'll get there in a minute, but we need to camp on that "very good[ness]." Sometimes, the story told by Christians is a subbiblical narrative in which creation itself is somehow evil. Our bodies are fleshly prisons that our immortal souls must escape. The world is a dump we are going to be raptured out of. We are all in Plato's cave, but one day Jesus will carry us out into a transcendent world of immaterial forms and disembodied spirits.

But this view is not biblical, and inasmuch as we believe it, we are actually blaspheming God's assessment of the world. And choosing to see the world as evil and focusing only on our escape from it is destructive to healthy grief. Failing to recognize creation's goodness leads us to make light of the sadness we feel when we lose part of it. Our tears are dismissed as an overattachment to dirty, material stuff.

If you have been taught the creation-is-bad idea, know that it is not the story of Scripture. The sorrow you feel when something is wrong in the world or someone is snatched away—that is a proper sorrow. Bodies are not meant to break down or decay, souls are not meant to be ripped from them in death, and the good things of this world are not meant to be taken from us. Anyone who so cheapens our loss is taking issue with the God who declared "very good" over what we grieve.

All Deeply Broken

God made everything good. At the same time, things aren't that simple anymore. The universe has been fractured by sin. In our rebellion against God, we have left this good world in tatters, a casualty of our war against heaven. Now creation is under a curse, and our relationship with it is not what it was meant to be. The apostle Paul pictures the world as crying out in distress: "We know that the whole creation has been groaning together in the pains of childbirth until now" (Romans 8:22). The destruction and darkness that surround us are in fact the agonized cries of a world abused. In the next verses, Paul paints our own pain as part of creation's groaning. The anguish we feel is an echo of the cosmic scream that has continued ever since we left Eden. Disease and disaster, injury and folly are all natural parts of life in this fallen age. Let's zoom in on the moment where things fall apart—what Christians call "the Fall." Adam and Eve are placed in Eden as its overseers (Genesis 1:26-28). In that place, they have a job to do, "to work . . . and keep" the garden (Genesis 2:5, 15) and, as they someday have children, to fill the earth and spread Eden across the world (Genesis 1:28). This work was not the drudgery of survival. The Lord provided for Adam and Eve's needs with unimaginable abundance (Genesis 2:16). There was only one commandment that came with this abundance: not to eat of "the tree of the knowledge of good and evil" (Genesis 2:17).

Thanks to the Sunday-school retellings of this story, we can get the wrong impression about God's command. We focus on the tree and its fruit as if there were some bad juju in the apples (or pears or whatever) themselves. In Scripture, the tree was not so much the problem as what *the act of eating from it* represented. While part of the serpent's temptation is that the fruit looks desirable to eat, the core rests in his promise that "when you eat of it your eyes will be opened, and you will be like God" (Genesis 3:5). Adam and Eve have a good place in God's good world, but in their sin, they abandon their right position and instead seek to become gods themselves.

What results is the breaking of every dimension of their lives. Their rebellion shatters their relationship with God. Instead of walking with him in the garden, now they hide from him (Genesis 3:8). They turn against each other. A once-loving marriage becomes a race to shift the blame. God asks Adam what he did. Adam's response is to point at "the woman whom you gave to be with me"—no longer "bone of my bones and flesh of my flesh" (Genesis 3:12; 2:23). At an even deeper level, Adam and Eve were turned against themselves. Since their creation, they had been "naked and . . . not ashamed," an expression of freedom and a sense of peace with who they are (Genesis 2:25). After their rebellion, they were ashamed and sought to hide who they were, not just from God but also from themselves (Genesis 3:7). Even their relationship to creation changed. Their calling to be fruitful and multiply, to work and tame the earth, comes under a curse. Childbearing becomes a source of pain, labor turns to toil, and the ground itself rebels (Genesis 3:16-17).

When God first warns Adam and Eve against eating from the tree, he warns them that if they eat of it, they "shall surely die" (Genesis 2:17). Adam and Eve aren't instantly struck down, but this is because the punishment in view is something much worse than simply the end of their physical lives. The curse speaks to a deeper death, a relational and metaphysical and spiritual perishing. All of the dimensions of sin we have named are included in this dying, and ultimately, they all feed into that final consequence: human mortality.

[God said,] "By the sweat of your face
    you shall eat bread,
till you return to the ground,
    for out of it you were taken;
for you are dust,
    and to dust you shall return."

GENESIS 3:19

This broad understanding of brokenness speaks to the breadth of our sorrow. Our world is everywhere colored by dying. There are a thousand griefs in life, and all of them are caught up in this story. The man who hides in shame because of ways he has been abused as a child, the woman for whom work is a frustration, the couple wounding each other in marital dysfunction and the one struggling with infertility, people trapped in civil wars, and those hiding in guilt from God—this is a story that includes all of their struggles.

Christians sometimes feel tempted to minimize or dismiss certain kinds of suffering or reduce them only to spiritual maladies without appreciating the all-encompassing nature of the Fall. Genesis teaches us otherwise. Nothing in this world is as it should be. Every dimension of human existence is touched by sin and the destruction it has caused.

Glorious Ruins

The brokenness does not negate the goodness of creation. Scripture still gives praise to God for its bounty and beauty (Psalms 8; 104). Through creation, we can still get a glimpse of the power and provision of God (Psalm 19:1-6; Romans 1:19-20).

I once walked through an abandoned, broken-down church in the country. It had been decades since anyone had used the place for anything more than storage for farm equipment. The walls were netted with vines. The stained glass was splattered with mud and missing pieces. The floor was warped, and patches of earth peeked through. It was a touching and tragic scene. You could imagine the songs of the saints that once echoed off the rafters, yet those rafters now sagged with water and age. The altar rail had been lovingly carved, perhaps the work of some pious craftsman, but now it was dented and hung with rusted chains. There was a sense of deep goodness in the place, but also of deep loss.

The theologian Francis Schaeffer reportedly described human beings as "glorious ruins." This is an apt description of our condition and indeed of our world. When we look around, we catch echoes of the goodness, yet it is that very goodness that makes the destruction so tragic. The beauty and the brokenness magnify each other, each showing the other clearer by contrast.

Almost all biblical teachings can be understood in terms of tension. A tension is not a contradiction—Scripture is not at odds with itself. Neither is it nonsense. A tension rests between two teachings that make sense in themselves but that pull against each other in our hearts and minds.

We live in a world that is very good and very broken. These two truths are in tension not because they contradict each other but because we struggle to hold them in balance. The human heart naturally gravitates toward one or the other. As a result, we constantly have to remind ourselves of the side of the story we are neglecting. When we are burdened by brokenness, we must cling to the beauty. When we relish the goodness, we must remain mindful of the mess.

This is especially true while feeling grief. Because of the pain, our tendency during suffering is to only see one side of the equation. This is certainly what happens when we spiral toward depression and despair. The dark part of our lives can swell and swallow up the light around it. The joy we once found in friends, in hobbies, in children, and in a sunny August afternoon are masked in shadow. However, we can also err in the other direction. Too often, the world's solution to pain is to just try not to think about it, to pretend like the sorrow isn't there. This denial leads us to be dismissive of others and to cut off parts of ourselves.

This side of Eden, we must endeavor to name the awful truth of our condition and at the same time recognize the beauty still lingering in the ruins. How do we do that? Given how overwhelming grief can feel, how can we have eyes able to behold both realities at once? We've already gotten a hint.

We recognize the world's goodness in the context of the God who made it. That is part of why Genesis 1 bears the structure it does. God's testimony about creation teaches us how to view it. At the same time, God's goodness pours from him into what he makes. We cannot properly celebrate creation without celebrating the Creator.

Likewise, the world's brokenness flows out of the broken relationship between humanity and God. It is not just that the Fall has a Godward dimension. The breach in our relationship with God causes all the other heartbreaks of our sin. Our move to overthrow him, to seek to become gods ourselves, was ground zero for the explosion of sorrow into the world. Our broken communities, our broken bodies, and our broken planet are all fallout from our rebellion. The way we think about both beauty and brokenness rests in how we think about God.

I have no intention to suggest that fixing our relationship with God will somehow fix our circumstances. That is the garbage peddled by some false shepherds: "You take care of stuff with God, and God will take care of your problems."

Nor will strengthening our relationship with him prevent us from experiencing deep sorrow. Jesus came as God himself, in perfect communion with the Father, and was betrayed, beaten, and killed for it, and he told his disciples they should pretty much expect the same (John 15:18-20).

However, I do believe that the key to walking through grief in a way that doesn't destroy us lies in how we think about and live before the Lord. Every defective way we deal with sadness rests on a defective understanding of God and his promises. Seeing God in his glory and compassion and complexity is central to finding healing for these defects and moving toward wholeness.

Scripture helps us see this complexity, offering four different pictures of God in our grief. Our issue is not so much that we don't believe any of them but that we usually hold only one or two. Without all four together, we end up with a warped view of God and of ourselves. With that as our goal, let's turn from this beautiful and broken world and contemplate how we see the one who made it and upholds it and will ultimately remake it.

PART II

God above Us

Sorrow is like sitting in a car as it sinks into the ocean. Everything seems almost normal: the worn seats, the gummy handle of the gearshift, the jumble of papers in the glove box. Yet water is dribbling out of the vents and around the doors. As the car descends into the depths, cracks start forming on the windows. The frame groans beneath the pressure. You are still dry, but every breath comes with the knowledge that the inky void is all around. In the next moment, the windshield might shatter, and the ocean will crush and suffocate you all at once.

The root of the English word grief *is an archaic French word for "to burden," which itself comes from the Latin word for* heavy. *In sorrow, everything is given unbelievable weight. Life exists under pressure. The effort it takes to smile, to move, seems resisted by an invisible force.*

I am slowly being crushed beneath the load. I try to be strong, but human strength has limits. My muscles are woven of finite chords. If I am to survive this, I need something beyond me to strengthen me. Something to push back against the waters of despair.

3

HE SITS
ENTHRONED

GROWING UP in the landlocked middle of the United States, I didn't enter the ocean until I was a teenager. I still remember my first time. With the overconfidence born of lessons at a small-town pool and the bravado of a young man in the presence of attractive girls, I plunged right in. Strolling through the surf, I did my best to pretend like this was an everyday thing. When the surf hit my face and I tasted the organic saltiness, I smiled. I kept swimming out to the buoys like I had something to prove, which, at that age, was absolutely the case. At last I turned, saw how far I was from shore, and transformed from a cocky adolescent into Peter on the water, realizing the place my ego had brought me.

I was suddenly overwhelmed with the vastness of the sea.

My skin seemed to stretch outward, merging with the cerulean infinity. It wasn't the danger of the ocean that shook me, not exactly. I knew about riptides and had seen plenty of shark documentaries, but I wasn't afraid of drowning or spotting a menacing fin. My terror came from something deeper. I knew that the ocean was an entity larger than I could comprehend. It was unknowable and unconquerable and could swallow all my hubris and ambition and achievements in an instant, its currents unslowed. I stroked back to shore faster than my pride likes to admit.

To this day, I feel a sliver of that terror when I swim in the sea. I've learned to keep the fear beneath the level of conscious thought, but the niggling dread is still there. I've heard the same thing from the few people I've met who make their living from the ocean, those who are in the navy or who reap its harvest. As much as they treat the ocean as familiar, as much as they romanticize it, somewhere in the background is the knowledge that it is a mistress too alien and mighty to truly tame.

This is the place we must begin when we think about God.

Scripture compares God to the sea. It uses the ocean as a picture of the enormity of his presence and providence: "Deep calls to deep at the roar of your waterfalls; all your breakers and your waves have gone over me" (Psalm 42:7). The vast waters are an analogy for his own vastness, as when Psalm 104 pictures the beams of his house as spanning its shores. Most often, the sea illustrates the enormity of God's understanding and control—the ocean itself is inconsequential before him, just one among his subjects: "Or who shut in the sea with doors when it burst out from the womb . . . and said, 'Thus far shall you come, and no farther, and here shall your proud waves be stayed'?" (Job 38:8, 11).

The sea is beyond us. We have explored only 5 percent of its floor.[1] There are whole continents' worth of geography no human eye has seen. More than that, the very act of trying to understand the ocean threatens our humanity. To probe it requires traversing airless depths at pressures that would pop us like grapes. To confront the sea is to confront a vastness that proves our frailty.

God comes with a power and a mystery that makes the Pacific look like a backyard puddle. That feeling of unsettling dread in the face of the ocean's vastness is a gesture in the direction of what Scripture calls the fear of the Lord (see Psalm 33:8; Ecclesiastes 12:13).

Complicating Our View of God

There is perhaps no other Old Testament prophet who writes with the grandeur and scope of Isaiah. In the first part of his book, Isaiah is focused on God's coming judgment against his people. The conclusion of chapter 39 is a foreboding warning of Israel's imminent conquest by Babylon, when all her greatest treasures will be carried away to decorate the palace of a foreign king.

Then the focus shifts. The prophet no longer warns of coming judgment but now offers comfort after judgment has come. He begins to speak a message of hope and restoration:

Comfort, comfort my people, says your God.
Speak tenderly to Jerusalem,
   and cry to her
that her warfare is ended,
   that her iniquity is pardoned,
that she has received from the LORD's hand
   double for all her sins.

ISAIAH 40:1-2

The rest of the book is a lengthy attempt to help Israel find peace and a new identity amid her grief. There are still warnings, but the overall tone is one of encouragement rather than impending doom. Isaiah speaks of God's protection, paints a picture of his suffering servant that bears our sins, and ultimately promises a new heaven and new earth where peace reigns.

Before all of that, though, the prophet calls Israel to "behold your God" (Isaiah 40:9). What are they to see? That God is vast and beyond searching out. Isaiah 40:12 pictures God cupping his hands to measure the enormity of the oceans. Nations and continents are but a scattering of dust to him (Isaiah 40:15). These pictures serve to remind us that God is far greater than we could ever aspire to be:

It is he who sits above the circle of the earth,
   and its inhabitants are like grasshoppers.

ISAIAH 40:22

Beholding God's greatness is an essential first step in the comfort Isaiah intends to bring. It is only by confronting our God enthroned above the heavens that we can begin to grasp the good news of God bent near in love.

If we are to follow the example of Isaiah, we need to make things harder before we make them easier. We need to complicate the way many of us view God, to make him someone we in a sense fear before he can comfort us. This might seem like a strange place to begin, and I want to acknowledge it might be hard for some of us. Yet it is also necessary. We must behold the majesty of God. If we do not appreciate his greatness, his goodness will prove a paltry thing.

Sovereignty

Perhaps the most challenging idea in Scripture is its insistence that God is in control even over the circumstances of our grief. The tendency of some in the church, whether implicitly or explicitly, is to pretend that God is helpless when it comes to the hard stuff. We see him as active in miraculous healing and acts of deliverance. When things go unexpectedly well, we say, "God really showed up." But when it comes to the painful things we experience, we feel the need to remove him. God could take the cancer from my wife, people seem to believe, but something else chose to allow the tumors to grow.

Scripture pictures God as sovereign. He is in control of everything that happens in the world. He is the one who "works all things according to the counsel of his will" (Ephesians 1:11). The psalmist tells us that "God is in the heavens; he does all that he pleases" (Psalm 115:3). The prophet Daniel gives this summary of God's rule:

> All the inhabitants of the earth are accounted as nothing,
>   and he does according to his will among the host
>   of heaven
>   and among the inhabitants of the earth;
>   and none can stay his hand
>   or say to him, "What have you done?"
> DANIEL 4:35

Let's not miss the implications of these claims because of their broadness: The Bible explicitly ties God's sovereignty to the things that make us uncomfortable. God is in control of terrible things that happen in the world, including disasters and human sickness (Job 2:10; Isaiah 45:7; Lamentations 3:37-38; Amos 3:6). God is in control of the plans and choices of human beings, including plans to do evil (Proverbs 19:21; 20:24; 21:1; Romans 9:17-18; James 4:13-15). God is in control of our deaths, including when and how they come (Deuteronomy 32:39; 1 Samuel 12:6; Job 14:5; Psalm 139:16). If this is a new idea, I would encourage you to pause and read through that list of texts to appreciate the picture Scripture gives.

In our modern world, few people acknowledge the reality of the parts of Scripture that show God exercising this kind of reign. I remember a youth retreat in my teens where the speaker explicitly said that God's control didn't extend to human evil, to natural disasters, to diseases, or even to unfortunate coincidences. "You shouldn't blame God for those things," he said, "because they aren't up to him." On the car ride home, I pressed our youth pastor on it. He said it seemed like we didn't want God to be in control of those things because we might end up mad at him. This is not how Scripture speaks. Scripture insists that God is sovereign—but that truth sometimes gets lost in our desire to make things not his fault.

Now, there are a few clarifications we need to make about Scripture's view of God's control. James 1:13 says that God does not tempt us to sin, and God's general portrait of righteousness in the Bible should also cause us to be careful about how we see God's sovereignty working out. There are certain things (like human evil) that God rules over without causing directly. We are still responsible beings who make real choices, not marionettes or robots. Our understanding of God's rule needs to be nuanced. However, we often focus so much on the nuance, we ignore the general reality of God's sovereignty.

Here is the truth, according to the Bible: God reigns over all the earth, that which is good and that which is evil. His reign does not always work the same way—he does not force people to sin against their own will, for example—but it is still real. He gives life, and he puts to death. He kills, and he heals. Nothing happens except what he is ultimately in control of. If my wife's cancer disappears tomorrow and never returns, God was sovereign over that. If it continues to grow until it kills her, God is sovereign over that as well.

Incomprehensibility

To one hard truth—that God is sovereign, no exceptions—
we must add another. In the book of Job, we see a righteous
man suffering horribly. We are told, in the opening chapters
of the book, that this suffering was a result of God allowing
Satan to test Job, but Job doesn't know that. All Job knows
is that he has sought to live a good life and, in the blink of
an eye, his wealth and his family and his health have all been
snatched away.

Understandably, amid this struggle, Job wants answers
from God. He asks the questions we all ask when we hurt.
He wants to know the "whys." Ultimately, he demands an
audience with God: "I would speak to the Almighty, and I
desire to argue my case with God" (Job 13:3). This desire to
reason with the Lord becomes almost a fantasy.

> Oh, that I knew where I might find him,
>   that I might come even to his seat!
> I would lay my case before him
>   and fill my mouth with arguments.
> I would know what he would answer me
>   and understand what he would say to me.
>
> JOB 23:3-5

You can sense he has played the scene over and over in his
mind, perfecting his arguments and covering every conceiv-
able angle.

Job's desire is treated with respect and a degree of

sympathy. Certainly, his heart cry for answers is better than the trite comfort of his friends. Honesty is viewed much more kindly than platitudes. However, when God descends at the end of the book, he doesn't come with the explanation Job desires. Instead God comes in a whirlwind and proceeds to ask a series of challenging questions of Job: "Where were you when I laid the foundation of the earth? Tell me, if you have understanding. Who determined its measurements—surely you know! Or who stretched the line upon it?" (Job 38:4-5). The list goes on: *Do you bring the rain? Do you know the lives of the remotest animals? Do you give the horse strength and the hawk flight?* Finally, after several chapters of such queries, the litany ends, and Job responds, "I know that you can do all things, and that no purpose of yours can be thwarted. 'Who is this that hides counsel without knowledge?' Therefore I have uttered what I did not understand, things too wonderful for me, which I did not know" (Job 42:2-3). Job doesn't get to plead his case; what he is left with after encountering God is a profound sense of his limitedness and folly.

When we confront God, we are in the presence of a being who is incomprehensible. By the very nature of who he is and what we are, we cannot understand him. The Lord is mysterious not by choice but by nature. God is like the mystery of the universe itself: We cannot grasp such vastness because we lack the capacity.

The fatal flaw in Job's arguments is the notion that God is the sort of being we can argue with in the first place. To have a debate, we need to have common ground. We need to be on roughly the same level. But God is not like us. My children are not well-equipped to render judgments on my decisions; that's why I'm their parent. Our guinea pigs are even less equipped. The further the distance between us, the more we must take on trust, and I am infinitely closer to my guinea pigs than I am to the Almighty.

Some of us have this idea that the reason God doesn't explain his actions is that he wants us to take them on faith. That someday it will all make sense—he'll sit us down in heaven and talk it through, and we'll nod and say, "Yes, I approve." That is not the Bible's understanding of God's will. God's mysteriousness is not an affectation or a test but a necessity. If God chose to explain himself, our tiny skulls would explode. A single thought in the mind of God is infinite, and all the brains of all humanity working together could not begin to contain it. He knows all things at once, future and past and present. He knows what will happen to me tomorrow and numbers the hairs on Julius Caesar's balding head and is watching every dust mote in every crater on planets orbiting distant stars we haven't even dreamed of, all at once.

The apostle Paul, after writing an eleven-chapter treatise on God's plan for the salvation of the world, ends in full recognition of this reality:

> Oh, the depth of the riches and wisdom and
> knowledge of God! How unsearchable are his
> judgments and how inscrutable his ways!

"For who has known the mind of the Lord,
 or who has been his counselor?"
"Or who has given a gift to him
 that he might be repaid?"

For from him and through him and to him are all
things. To him be glory forever. Amen.
ROMANS 11:33-36

The more we understand God's incomprehensible majesty, the more Paul's words become our prayer as well: "Your
ways are inscrutable. Your judgments are unsearchable. You
are the source and ruler and purpose of all things. Amen."
We turn from trying to explain and argue and understand
and instead fall into the silence of small creatures before their
eternal Creator.

Evil and Suffering

Here we must pause to talk about a question almost everyone
asks at some point in grief. What about the "problem of evil"?
If God is good and all-powerful, how can evil and suffering
exist?

At times this is an emotional question, wrought by agony.
God, where are you? Are you even there? In this sense, the problem of evil represents a normal, human struggle. Scripture is
full of such cries of doubt. This book is about wrestling with
these feelings. If you are there, what we're about to discuss
isn't really aimed at you. We'll delve into those things later.

However, for other people, the problem of evil becomes a philosophical issue. It is not a groaning of the heart but a question for our minds. This doesn't mean we should ignore it. We can get hung up on such doubts if we don't take the time to work through them.

At its simplest, that question boils down to a single set of premises and a conclusion: (*a*) God is good; (*b*) God is all-powerful; (*c*) a good God would not allow evil and suffering in the world; (*d*) an all-powerful God could prevent it; (*e*) evil and suffering exist; therefore, such a God cannot. While that sounds persuasive, it is rarely stated so simply because a bit of reflection makes us realize there are significant issues with *c* and *d*.

There are any number of reasons why a good God might allow some amount of suffering. Free will, opportunities to learn and overcome adversity, the shaping and maturing effect that pain can have in our lives, and just responses to human sin—these things do not remove the evilness of evil, but they create space for us to understand why God might allow it.

The more persuasive form of the argument deals not with evil as a general idea but either with the amount of it or with specific examples of it. *Surely*, it says, *while some suffering might be understandable, this much of it cannot make sense.* My heart resonates with that case; we should weep at the extent to which the world is broken. It is right and human to wrestle with the depths of what is wrong with the world.

However, this argument runs into problems because of

what we just said about God's incomprehensibility. To pass judgments on his decisions, God must be a being we can understand. He isn't. All we have really proven is that a God we can comprehend doesn't exist, and that is something to which Scripture would say, "Amen."

So why does the argument still feel so persuasive? One of the hardest things about Christianity is that it forces us into a posture of humility. For centuries, humans have assumed that our minds are the greatest forces in the universe. There is no puzzle they cannot solve, no paradox they cannot unravel. We have demanded that God be rational and deferential and quick to explain himself. When he isn't, we assume he must be the one in the wrong.

But before the Living God, our assumptions are revealed as self-delusions. We are Adam and Eve in the garden all over again, thinking that by eating the fruit of knowledge, we can become as gods. In truth, when compared to the Almighty, we are unbelievably small. We have less grasp of the Lord than I have of the depth and breadth of the Atlantic. We cannot contain him, cannot move him, and will never fully know him. If we try, we will be sucked beneath the surface of the sea.

God Is Bigger than This

The day we discovered Elizabeth had cancer was brutal. Usually, there are hints ahead of time that something is coming, periods of waiting and uncertainty. We have experienced those times in the years since, but her original diagnosis landed like a flurry of blows. She had gone in for a colonoscopy because of minor symptoms which could have had numerous more likely, less serious explanations. We dropped her off and made plans for me and the kids to pick her up afterward. We were planning to get drinks with some friends that evening. However, over a few hours, we learned that she had a very large tumor growing through the wall of her intestines and that, thanks to the tumor, the colonoscopy had caused a tear that was flooding bacteria into her abdomen. She went into emergency surgery that night, both to remove the growth and to stitch up her digestive system. The next morning, still less than a day in, we were told that cancer had spread into other parts of her body and the prognosis was not good.

The stress and worry that would usually have filled several weeks was packed into half a day. As she was being taken away to surgery that evening and I was left to wait, I stumbled into the hospital chapel. It was nothing special— a flower-wreathed altar and an obviously fake stained-glass window facing some padded pews—but at that moment, it was a place where I could seek the presence of God. I was a wreck. I couldn't pray anything beyond a mumbled, "Please let her be okay." Mostly, I just reeled under the enormity of it all. I had no idea what the future held beyond the awful certainty it would involve a lot of pain.

Kneeling against the wooden altar, staring at the colored patterns on the floor, I was not comforted by hollow promises. There wasn't space in my brain to think through the future. I wasn't seeking to parse meaning. I wasn't wrestling with God's will. I was simply crushed under the weight of the last eight hours. Yet as anguish pressed me down, I found a deep reality pressing me back up at the same time:

God is greater than this.

That was the truth the Spirit drove into my mind. While I am not prone to mystical experiences, I found my imagination drawn upward, picturing one striding across the stars with infinite wisdom in his eyes and unstoppable power in his right hand. This was not the image I would have expected; it certainly wasn't the one I as a pastor would first run to when consoling someone experiencing grief. Yet it was exactly what I needed.

Staring at that phantasm of glory, what seeped through my consciousness was the truth that my wife's cancer was not the greatest power in the universe. We were not helpless victims of the chaos of mutating cells, the losers of some cosmic lottery. While our world was falling to pieces, God was still sovereign, ordaining where each piece would land. While our dreams for the future had collapsed, his plans for the world and for our lives had not changed a bit. The Lord was still the Lord, and because of that fact, my fear lost some of its power. Nothing about our situation was changed, but my racing heart slowed as I beheld the one who was on the throne.

Scripture often contrasts the fear of things in the world with the fear of God. Somehow, part of what delivers us from our terror over life circumstances or human evil or our broken world is the deeper terror we feel when confronted by God's vastness. That is what I experienced in that chapel. I could not, knowing my wife was being cut open and her guts pulled out, make sense of the truth that God loved me. Not in that moment. God's love was important, but it came later. The place I had to start was the more basic reality that God was God. The powers of cancer and death were nothing before him. That is where we must begin in our sorrow. God is greater than our grief and pain. He is greater than us.

4

GLORY AND PURPOSE

I'D LOVE TO SAY that the story of how I married Elizabeth was like a Hollywood romance, but nothing could be further from the truth. We met in college, as members of a campus ministry I quit a few months later. There was no shaft of light from the heavens or scattering of rose petals. I first got to know her through shared social circles and, later, a vague crush I had on one of her friends. Over several years, we grew to appreciate each other, and that appreciation grew into affection, but it was not puppy-dog love when I asked her out to dinner.

If I wasn't head over heels, Elizabeth had both feet firmly on the ground. She came from a place in Bible-church evangelical Christianity that viewed dating with intensity: the first date was the climax of years of agonizing prayer, and the second tantamount to a marriage proposal. I tried to tell her that I didn't mean it that way, but she still felt like she had to pray about it for a week before agreeing to a second dinner. At the end of that time, she told me, "Well, I'm not really interested in you or attracted to you at all, but if you really want to take me out again knowing that, I guess I'd say yes."

Four months later, we got engaged, and three months after that, we got married.

Elizabeth was twenty-three when we got married; I was twenty-one and still had a year of college left. While I'm sure our ages and the whirlwind nature of our romance raised eyebrows, I became a huge fan of being married young. It gave us a sense of stability and purpose our lives had lacked up to that point. Home was a refuge where I could rest and study and a place where we could invite friends to share and practice hospitality. We were able to engage with the world in new ways as a married couple.

When you marry young, everything else in life gets caught up in your union. While we've always given each other space to pursue our private interests, we never had the opportunity to build separate lives. Our friendships and choices and experiences have always been intertwined. My choice to pursue the ministry, her decisions about work, and our discussions about family were made together. We would often look at elderly couples who seemed to have grown to be halves of a whole and joke that we were well on our way.

All these realities were shattered when we received Elizabeth's terminal diagnosis. We had already been battling cancer for several years at that point, but when her oncologist uttered the word *incurable* and started discussing the prognosis in spans you could count on your hands, everything turned upside down. What most disoriented me as we received the bad news wasn't the practical or emotional challenges of losing my wife. Instead, it was that my whole picture of the future had been upended. It isn't that I had no identity beyond our marriage; for all our intertwinement, both of us have always had a strong conviction that we need other passions besides each other to have a healthy sense of who we are in our relationship.

But even so—everything was colored by my love for Elizabeth. She was the sun around which everything else orbited, and without her, the planetoids of my life seemed to career off in every direction.

Grief often presents as a low-grade depression. Not something that requires a clinical diagnosis—although for some people, it grows into that and needs the help of a professional—but a general malaise that weaves through the fabric of existence. You are on a path, moving through the world, but suddenly the ground seems to shift and you're not sure which way is forward.

Mourning a loss is not an event but a journey. One of the realities of that journey is that some answers are only helpful once we reach a place where we need them. Trying to put everything into the backpack at the start just drags us down.

In the first searing moments of grief, what we need is not a sense of purpose but of comfort and presence. We should feel the things we feel and rage over what is gone and weep a bunch and let ourselves be numb. It is crucial to allow yourself to feel those things because they are true. If you are reading this book and are in this first place, I'd encourage you to skip what follows and go on to the next two sections, as I think they offer more of the resources you will need.

That said, while those feelings never fully disappear, the moment will come, perhaps even soon, when you must move forward. When questions like *Why should I get out of bed?* seem monumental but must be answered and life must be lived. We have been dwelling under a Damocles's sword of terminal illness, but we cannot just wait for years until the end.

Our vision of God on the throne provides a resource like no other for moving forward under the weight of grief. Understanding who we are in relation to an exalted God helps us reclaim our identity. He provides the context within which the pieces of our broken hearts can still find their places.

The Glory of the Lord

Our culture, as we've discussed, struggles to confront death and grief. An obsession with self-fulfillment and self-expression cannot survive the undoing of the self. Christians don't always do a good job of providing a better answer. Our tendency is to think that Christianity's answer to the question of purpose in the face of death is heaven. Too often, both secular people (dismissively) and religious people (piously) pretend like the solution to loss rests purely in a future escape from this world. Mortality is just a probationary period before our true lives begin.

While there is an important place for the afterlife, this approach is destructive. The idea of heaven can make me feel better about the end of suffering, but it cannot help me live beneath its weight. I remember, as a young person, asking a pastor why Christians shouldn't simply commit suicide. We should get this purgatorial age over with and get on with eternity. The question understandably alarmed him, but it wasn't that I was considering such an act. I just couldn't understand the reason to engage with life, given the escapist theology I had been given. His answer wasn't much help. It amounted to telling me that God would be quite unhappy with us if we started killing ourselves, and besides, there were souls to save. Which is true, I suppose, but it leaves a lot to be desired in terms of a positive vision for life. Any system of values that boils down to "keep living because God will be disappointed if you don't" does not inspire greatness.

Heaven, while a sweet *hope* when properly understood, is not the *purpose* of the Christian life. It is a good thing to live in light *of* but an insufficient thing to be living *for*. To understand the reason this is true, we need to step back and ask the bigger question cultures are really answering when they confront death: What do we exist for? What is the point of it all?

One of the passages I often turn to for comfort is Isaiah 43. It begins with this sweet promise of the Lord's salvation:

But now thus says the LORD,
he who created you, O Jacob,
   he who formed you, O Israel:
"Fear not, for I have redeemed you;
   I have called you by name, you are mine."

ISAIAH 43:1

So we have God speaking to his people as their Creator and their Redeemer. After communicating his love, God promises to sustain his people through their troubles:

When you pass through the waters, I will be with you;
   and through the rivers, they shall not overwhelm you;
when you walk through fire you shall not be burned,
   and the flame shall not consume you.

ISAIAH 43:2

All of which is a comfort we will consider later, but it doesn't get at the reason God promises this care. That waits until a few verses later. God has already pointed to the fact that he created his people. He also joined that, in verse 1, with the easy-to-overlook remark that "I have called you by name." What does that mean? The end of this passage returns to that phrase, helping us understand:

everyone who is called by my name,
   whom I created for my glory,
whom I formed and made.

ISAIAH 43:7, EMPHASIS MINE

Being called by God's name is a picture of our purpose. We exist not for ourselves but to magnify the name, the reputation, of God. We were created for the glory of God, Isaiah says, and this is the reason for God's work of salvation. Isaiah repeatedly stresses this fact in the following chapters. God rescued Israel in order "that they might declare [his] praise" (Isaiah 43:21). God rescues so that he "will be glorified in Israel" (Isaiah 44:23). This culminates in Isaiah 48, which makes the idea so explicit that only the most strenuous of mental gymnastics can avoid it:

For my name's sake I defer my anger;
   for the sake of my praise I restrain it for you,
      that I may not cut you off.
Behold, I have refined you, but not as silver;
   I have tried you in the furnace of affliction.
For my own sake, for my own sake, I do it,
   for *how should my name be profaned?*
      My glory I will not give to another.

ISAIAH 48:9-11, EMPHASIS MINE

Isaiah's point is inescapable: God's purpose, and the purpose of his people, is his glory.

The New Testament echoes this theme that we are meant to glorify God. Paul says it to the church in Corinth, reminding them of the purpose that should undercut their petty squabbles: "So, whether you eat or drink, or whatever you do, do all to the glory of God" (1 Corinthians 10:31). Jesus states it in the Sermon on the Mount as our motivation for good works: "In the same way, let your light shine before others, so that they may see your good works and give glory to your Father who is in heaven" (Matthew 5:16). Our whole reason for existence in the world is to give God glory, to draw forth praises for his name.

Struggling with Glory

This idea—that God's purpose and ours are ultimately to show forth his glory—makes us uncomfortable. One reason stems from the pernicious notion that we can think about God in roughly the same way we think about human beings. When a person is living only for his or her own glory, that is a bad thing. It makes us imagine the ball hog who shows off rather than being a team player, or the greedy heiress who thinks the world should revolve around her petty whims. God seeking his own glory seems to make him a cosmic egotist with a fragile sense of self-worth.

This area is one in which God is simply not like us. What is the issue with a human being seeking his or her own glory? It is that the world is not designed to sustain such a pursuit. The only way a human being can increase is by causing others to decrease. This leads glory-seeking humans to behave in ways that are destructive to others. In the case of God's glory, the opposite is the case. Creation in its intended goodness is a glory-reflecting machine. Its peace and bounty and beauty are the channels through which God's majesty flows out into the universe. The world working in the best possible way and God showing forth his glory are one and the same thing.

In addition, God's glory is different from ours in that it is fully deserved. Consider the person who is a ball hog. The problem is not that he is getting glory for what he does; it is that he is seeking more than he is due. When a skilled basketball player soars through the air to dunk the ball over the arms of a defender, that act deserves a certain response of awe. We should not begrudge the player our praise. The problem comes when the player is not content with what is warranted and instead seeks more than he's due, demanding the credit that should also go to his teammates and coaches. God cannot do this because all things are due to him.

God is glorious by his very nature. Why does he then call us to glorify him? Is God's grip on glory so tenuous that our failure to adequately notice somehow robs him of significance? We imagine him behaving like the insecure teenager who constantly demands that people validate their smallest achievements.

Again, the problem is thinking of God as an oversized human being. God does not need our praise (Psalm 50:8-15; Acts 17:25). It is not that we must give him glory in order to add something to him; rather, he calls us to seek his glory because it is what is best for us. We are a part of that chorus of creation, designed to gorgeously resonate with his praise.

Perhaps a different picture is necessary. Stop imagining God in terms of a human being. Instead, when we speak about God's glory, we are speaking of something more like the radiant light of the sun. Creativity and power and righteousness and wisdom unavoidably shine forth from him, simply because he is God. There is no need for arm-waving or attention-seeking. At the same time, our call to glorify him is nothing more than a calling to live in that life-giving light. Our job is one of reflection; the problem is not that God lacks light in himself but that when we refuse to be his mirrors, shadows enter the world and darkness increases.

Our Goal in Grief

How does God's glory meet our grief? We think that happiness is the goal of life, but happiness is a mediocre purpose. Those seeking it never accomplish much of worth. Given that life includes suffering and, ultimately, death, what we need is a purpose big enough to make that struggle worthwhile. We need something worth laboring for, and there is no worthier goal than God's glory embodied in our lives.

Pursuing the self cannot sustain us in the face of this world's brokenness. A pursuit of God's glory can. In fact, such a purpose is uniquely suited to creating people who are unafraid in the face of loss and sorrow. When our highest ambition is to show forth the goodness and love of God, we can do that just as fully in our dying as in our living, just as clearly in how we handle loss as in how we respond to gain. Jesus himself, in his prayer of preparation for the cross, prayed, "Father . . . glorify your Son that the Son may glorify you" (John 17:1).

I am not saying that suffering itself is good. The brokenness of the world is not the way things are meant to be. However, what God's glory provides is a purpose we can live into even in the rubble of humanity's fall. He hasn't stopped shining simply because our rebellion brought darkness into the story. In him, we can still find meaning and direction for our lives that no sorrow, not even death, can take away. The world can wound us, but it cannot rob us of our significance and purpose if they rest in the glory of the Lord.

In life, we will all face sorrows of many kinds. No magic spell can make them go away, no matter how much we might wish for one. Christianity does not offer such sorcery. However, while sorrow will always wound us, it does not have to break us. Life in God offers us a flourishing that can be found even in hardship—never the unqualified joy of a season of plenty, but something that nonetheless gives meaning and direction to our struggle. Sorrow leaves us undone only when we don't have a sense of meaning that transcends the pain. The question is not so much the size of our burden as the size of the reason we shoulder it and press forward.

While grief upsets the structure of our world, it does not change the goal of our lives. The apostle Paul, himself no stranger to painful experiences, says it like this: "None of us lives to himself, and none of us dies to himself" (Romans 14:7). That is the lie of our world: I am the goal of my life. Instead, Paul goes on, "If we live, we live to the Lord, and if we die, we die to the Lord. So then, whether we live or whether we die, we are the Lord's" (Romans 14:8).

We exist in this world to show forth the goodness and greatness of God. That calling is what gives us purpose and significance. It is meant to anchor our identity. It is a calling, as Paul says, that continues no matter our life circumstances. We live and we die to the Lord. This fact transforms grief from something we simply endure into something we can steward for good.

Because this calling rests on God rather than our own happiness or self-realization, our source of purpose is secure. If our purpose in life is built on our sense of identity, our pleasure, or even something as good as a spouse, it is always under threat because those things are unstable. They are part of a world that heaves and shakes with the effects of sin. However, God remains unchanged. He can supply us with meaning and direction even when the earth gives way.

Don't misunderstand. Finding our ultimate purpose in God's glory does not mean we don't invest in ourselves or our marriage or our work or our children. God does not pit himself against the good things of this world. However, he does alter the reasons we pursue them. He changes them from ultimate goals to opportunities to glorify him. I love and care for my wife not because she fulfills me or completes me or supports me but because God calls me to love her. I raise my children not because they are my identity but because I am seeking to help them find theirs in Christ. My work and my hobbies can be enjoyed but don't require me to invest them with more weight than they can bear.

One of the hard but necessary things I have recognized in our season of impending loss is that I have not always lived into this calling. There are ways I have used my marriage to serve my own need for meaning, and it has hurt my wife. All of us are guilty of this in different ways with different parts of life. The Bible calls these tendencies "idolatry." We place some created thing in a position of importance that belongs only to the Creator. When we do, we diminish ourselves and damage the object of our idolatry. No person in this world is meant to bear the burden of ultimate significance. It leaves us demanding a perfection and strength of them that undercuts the grace each of us needs in our weakness and failures. Only when our trust in our idols fails do we begin to see our need for a deeper purpose that rests in God.

A Series of Small, Hard Choices

God's glory provides an indestructible purpose. It is a powerful resource to help us move forward under the burden of sorrow. Yet even in writing these words, I feel like I'm doing an injustice to how it feels in practice. It can sound like some hagiographic account of a martyrdom, too romantic and unwavering for the hardscrabble realities of my heart.

In practice, living in this season is not some grandiose sweep of glory and more a series of small, hard choices. I must choose to do the next thing, to go to work and invest in the people God has called me to care for, to be present with my children, and to not withdraw from my marriage into myself. I must choose whether to lay on the couch in the evening or to get up and serve my family. I must persevere in making these choices, and there are plenty of times when I fail. Having a vision for God's glory does not mean there is some ball of energy in my chest that makes those choices easy. Many days feel like moving through a vat of molasses. What his glory provides, though, is a different perspective on what I am choosing in each of those moments.

One of the dangers of despair is that it can keep us from seeing the truth of our lives. It is like a shadowed lens between us and the world, making the good things invisible and casting the shadows in stark relief. The deeper we slip into this distorted vision, the less we are able to rouse ourselves. Faithfulness seems like a monumental effort for a result that doesn't seem worth the pain.

God's glory functions like a lighthouse to sailors lost at sea, a shining beacon by which we can navigate. It recasts our decisions: I am not taking care of myself because I am worthwhile (I don't feel worth much some mornings) but because God created me with significance and purpose. I engage with my wife not because it is worth the pain I know it will eventually bring but because God made me to serve her and, in doing so, to serve him. The glory of God changes the stakes. I might still choose the path of least resistance, but when I do, I am forced to recognize that there is a profound cost.

To put it another way, God's glory offers me a story I can inhabit even when the other stories in my life turn tragic. I love the story of how Elizabeth and I met and got married. I've shared it hundreds of times, and each repetition makes me look across at Elizabeth and smile, relishing the shared memories and the shape of her face. It is a wonderful story, but if it is *the* story of my life, then my life will be over when hers ends. What God offers is a larger narrative. Our life together is a major plot thread, a glorious act 2, but it is not the whole play. The reason the curtain rises comes from the Lord, and the play will continue even when my favorite companion disappears stage left and I am left alone.

PART III

God beside Us

Sorrow is like a shadowy monster that dwells at the edge of your vision. It doesn't have a distinct shape, only a darkness in the corner of your eye. Its presence, though, is inescapable. You know that if you turn to look, suddenly it will be able to strike, so that is the last thing you want to do. Better to keep it there, safely ignored . . . but what is that? A movement? Is it now becoming animate while unobserved? The only way to know is to glance, and at that glance, it lunges, claws outstretched.

Living with that shadow is exhausting. You don't even have to look on purpose. Sometimes it's just an accidental twitch of the eye that brings it to life. I am continually straining to look straight ahead. My environment is a minefield of accidental glances. I am harried and weary from the threat. I am running, yet I cannot flee.

Do you meet me in such places, Father? Can your strong right arm protect me from such an intangible foe? Its claws have raked me, its sinuous black tongue drains my strength. Is this at last the battle I must fight alone?

5

A MAN
OF SORROWS

THERE IS A STRANGE, sweet fellowship to be found in the community of the grieving. When we announced to our church that Elizabeth's cancer had returned, many people expressed anguish. There were offers of prayer and help. People wept with us, and we were glad for them all. However, the moment that touched us the most was when an elderly widow, still mourning her long-passed husband and herself peering over the lip of the grave, simply embraced my wife and said, "I am really looking forward to seeing Jesus. I know you are too." There was a knowledge in her sad eyes that left Elizabeth feeling seen.

I was speaking at an event for teenagers at our church. One of them, who had recently lost her father to a tragic and undiagnosed medical condition, approached me afterward. I was expecting her to ask for advice or an explanation or some nugget of pastoral wisdom I could share. Instead, with compassion in her voice, she said, "It's hard, right? But you'll make it through this." That shared moment meant more to me than the entire stack of encouraging letters on the counter at home.

One of the unexpected blessings we have discovered in the land of cancer is the fellow travelers. My wife, with a newly shaved head, is stopped in a supermarket lot by another young woman with a similar diagnosis. Their shared grief instantly connects them, and a chance encounter turns into a lasting friendship. A guy I hardly know reaches out, facing a hard diagnosis for his own family, so that we can sit in it together. Our shared silences speak consolatory volumes. I visit elderly congregants for whom the youthful illusion of immortality shattered long ago, and we talk with a formerly-alien-to-me familiarity about the pains of this world.

Sorrow shared is a powerful bond. In the midst of our situation, I often find myself seeking those who know it. Normal conversations feel exhausting, trying to manage my own emotions and those of the other person. It feels like we are conversing in a foreign language I only half remember, each word requiring concentration and nothing coming out quite right. Talking with those who have suffered in significant ways is like slipping into my native tongue, both in the words and in the cavernous silences around them. "It sucks," I say, tired eyes tracing the cracks on the sidewalk. "Sure does," they respond, and in that brief interchange, we know and are known.

In the last two chapters, we discussed God in his exaltation.

That is a necessary perspective lest what follows be misunderstood, but left on its own, it leaves us with a distant deity. This distance becomes especially pronounced when we face sorrow. If I feel a gulf between me and human beings who haven't walked this road, how much more do I feel it with an ineffable God untouched by the broken state of his creation? How can he know? How can he understand the consequences of his sovereign decrees?

Sometimes my heart feels angry, wrestling with such questions. Sometimes it feels helpless and small. Yet here is the mystery I continue to discover: Even as I am shaking my fist at God as he sits in the heavens, I suddenly stub my toe and look down to find him here as well. One of the remarkable claims of Christianity is that while God is enthroned in the heavens, he has also drawn near to us. He is a fellow sufferer, a God who is beside us in our pain.

The Suffering Servant

The prophet Isaiah speaks to exiled Israel of God's coming salvation. He begins in a place we have already visited, declaring the universal rule of God:

> How beautiful upon the mountains
> > are the feet of him who brings good news,
> who publishes peace, who brings good news of happiness,
> > who publishes salvation,
> > who says to Zion, "Your God reigns."

ISAIAH 52:7

God is coming, baring his mighty arm before the nations, going out before and behind us as a defender, Isaiah says (Isaiah 52:10). He is sovereign and good, and this is Israel's hope in the face of her exile.

Then Isaiah's prophecy takes a strange turn. At the end of chapter 52, he begins to speak of a "servant" who will bring this salvation. This servant comes with God's power: "He shall be high and lifted up, and shall be exalted" (Isaiah 52:13). However, almost as soon as the servant appears, our expectations are upended. He will be exalted, but "his appearance was so marred, beyond human semblance, and his form beyond that of the children of mankind" that the earth was left to wonder (Isaiah 52:14). Behold your exalted king, disfigured beyond recognition: That is how Isaiah introduces his vision of God's coming salvation.

The way Isaiah paints this servant is jarring. While the servant comes to bring the rule of God, he does so not in glory but in anonymity: "He had no form or majesty that we should look at him, and no beauty that we should desire him" (Isaiah 53:2). More than that, he comes not just in humility but to face humiliation:

He was despised and rejected by men,
 a man of sorrows and acquainted with grief;
and as one from whom men hide their faces
 he was despised, and we esteemed him not.

ISAIAH 53:3

The core characteristic of this servant is his suffering. He was acquainted with grief; even more, he was despised for it. The people of God saw his brokenness and used it as evidence that he could not truly be of the Lord.

> Surely he has borne our griefs
>   and carried our sorrows;
> yet we esteemed him stricken,
>   smitten by God, and afflicted.
>
> ISAIAH 53:4

This verse begins to explain the reason for the servant's pain. His grief is not incidental or personal. It is redemptive suffering, an act of carrying the burden of our brokenness on his shoulders. At the same time, the fact that redemption is being worked through suffering causes those looking on to misunderstand. They can't imagine that this battered, bloody servant is an agent of God's salvation. These two themes together inform the rest of Isaiah's portrait. He goes on to tell us the servant is "pierced," "crushed," "wound[ed]," "oppressed," and "afflicted." All of this was both done for us and is the reason we failed to recognize in him the rule of God (Isaiah 53:5-7).

This image of the suffering servant is vivid, but if it existed in a vacuum, it might leave us confused. Is this an image for Israel in her captivity, or maybe the way the prophet Isaiah pictures his own ministry? Neither of those explanations accounts for the fact that Israel and Isaiah both seem to be the object, not the subject, of the servant's salvation. The "us" that runs through the prophecy includes both God's people as a whole and the prophet as one of their number, leaving the servant as a third actor in the play.

For Christians, the New Testament provides a clear answer to the identity of this servant. On the road to Gaza, Philip meets an Ethiopian eunuch who is reading this very passage. In response to the man's inquiries, "Philip opened his mouth, and beginning with this Scripture he told him the good news about Jesus" (Acts 8:35). Matthew cites Isaiah's words in connection with Jesus' ministry of healing (Matthew 8:17). Peter alludes to Isaiah's prophecy as being fulfilled at the cross: "He himself bore our sins in his body on the tree, that we might die to sin and live to righteousness. By his wounds you have been healed" (1 Peter 2:24). Jesus is the suffering servant, come to work salvation for his people through his own anguish and death.

The Dying Savior

There was a crucifix on the wall in the hospital room where my wife recovered after her first surgery, cheap stained wood superimposed with a metal casting of a slender man. It was probably mass-produced in a factory. The crucified man didn't hang right; he wasn't sagging enough under the gravity that would have slowly choked the air from his lungs. His face looked more like a pouting teenager than a guy with metal spikes through his wrists. Yet it was a symbol that stirred my heart.

In itself, the crucifix is a bizarre symbol to hang in a hospital. It is a portrait of a dying man in a place where people are desperately trying not to think about death. The agony of the cross is a reminder of what lurks just beyond the morphine haze. The inhumanity of the thing, the blood and sweat and mockery of it—nothing about the cross makes sense when everything else in this room tries to offer a clinical comfort.

Yet for all that, the cross is somehow a symbol of comfort. It is not simply a mark of man's brutality or of inescapable mortality but of something deeper. The cross carries with it the hope that somehow our suffering is transformed by the suffering of the one impaled on its wood.

We cannot understand Jesus Christ without recognizing how the cross stands at the apex of his ministry. It is certainly important to consider his moral teachings and miracles and manner of life. We ought to see in Jesus an example of faithfulness and a source of wisdom. However, from the start, Jesus' ministry operates in the shadow of his execution. It is there in his first miracle. "They have no wine" for the wedding feast, Mary tells her son. His cryptic protest? "My hour has not yet come" (John 2:3-4). He speaks of it often to his disciples, opening the Scriptures to explain that "the Son of Man must suffer many things and be rejected by the elders and the chief priests and the scribes and be killed" (Mark 8:31). As he prepares to go to Jerusalem for the final week of his life, Jesus makes clear that he is going as one knowing full well what will happen there: his betrayal, arrest, and crucifixion (Matthew 20:17-19).

Some people imagine Jesus' death as an unintended tragedy. They portray him as a wide-eyed prophet of peace who
accidentally runs afoul of tyrants and is ground beneath the
wheel of political power. However, all four firsthand accounts
of his life insist that Jesus approached the cross with inten-
tionality, seeing in it the culmination of his messianic mission. He was God's servant, and he knew full well that he
faced the suffering Isaiah spoke of centuries before.

The Gospels all slow down as they approach the final
week of Jesus' life. Biographies which before only hit the
high points zoom in, laboring over the final days and then,
at an even slower pace, the final hours. Jesus at the table,
sharing one last meal with his friends and trying, with the
bread and wine, to help them understand his sacrifice.
Jesus in the garden, sweating blood, those same friends not
even able to stay awake. Jesus betrayed by Judas, beaten,
ridiculed, and spat on. Jesus stumbling under the weight of
wood, battered and humiliated. Jesus dying, drawing ragged
breaths, speaking his final words. Jesus abandoned by his
Father. Jesus dead.

While every experience of suffering is unique, it is strik-
ing just how many facets were experienced by the Son of
God. He knew relational loss and loneliness, betrayal, injustice, physical pain, social humiliation, and spiritual isolation. Every species of anguish and struggle can be found in
his final days. All of which is particularly significant within
the Christian story—because it insists that Jesus was also
God.

The Divine Lamb

The book of Revelation is the apostle John's record of his prophetic vision from God. Some people try to read Revelation
as if it is some codebook about the future, which causes them
to miss the point. While there are elements of foretelling in
the book—Jesus hasn't returned yet, after all—most of John's
visions are meant instead to be an unveiling of the present.
His aim is to reveal the reality of our world.

Early in the vision, John is given a glimpse into the heavenly throne room. In that resplendent place sits the Father
and the heavenly court, but a third figure stands there as well.
He is announced as "the Lion of the tribe of Judah, the Root
of David" (Revelation 5:5). This is the language of the Jewish
Messiah, the hoped-for descendant of David who Christians
identify as Jesus. Yet when John looks for this lion, what he
sees instead is a lamb looking "as though it had been slain"
(Revelation 5:6). The text doesn't offer details, but perhaps
we can guess at them. Wool matted with dried blood. Scarred
slashes where wounds had been dealt.

Up until this point, those celestial creatures had only sung
praises to the one on the throne, but now they sing the same
praises to the Lamb, identifying him as God just as surely as
the Father. The heavenly court falls down before the Lamb,
pouring out the prayers of the saints at his feet: "You were
slain, and by your blood you ransomed people for God from
every tribe and language and people and nation" (Revelation
5:9). Jesus is not just a human being who suffered and died;
he is a divine being who reigns but who still bears the marks

of his suffering. Jesus isn't just a suffering servant; he is the suffering God.

We must not miss that there is a unity and equality between Jesus the Lamb and the Father on the throne. The juxtaposition is so shocking that we often pry them apart in our minds. Sometimes this is done by pitting Jesus the Son against God the Father. I was recently talking to a young woman who has faced profound loss in her life, and that was the move she made. "Jesus is great. I love Jesus," she said. "It's God that I have a problem with." This separation is a mistake. An understandable one, but nonetheless an error that costs us one of the most beautiful pieces of Christian hope: The Lamb is the Lord.

The God who is sovereign, Scripture says, is also the God who suffered. There is an unavoidable connection between the sovereignty and the suffering. Peter proclaims that Jesus was "delivered up according to the definite plan and fore-knowledge of God" (Acts 2:23). His betrayal and arrest were, as the apostles pray to God, what "your hand and your plan had predestined to take place" (Acts 4:28). In case we're tempted to read those passages and still try to make it only the Father's will, we are chastised by the words of Jesus himself: "No one takes [my life] from me, but I lay it down of my own accord. I have authority to lay it down, and I have authority to take it up again" (John 10:18).

This is a scandalous truth. God the King, the one who rules over all that happens in the earth, ordained that he himself would suffer and die. Jesus created the tree on which he would hang. He gave strength to the centurions' arms as they drove nails through his wrists. He appointed the rule of Herod and Pilate and all those who presided over his execution. God drained to the dregs the cup of punishment that he himself poured.

The God Who Knows Our Pain

This vision of a God who has himself suffered testifies to his mysterious but good character. God's suffering is part of the answer to that deeper, emotional struggle with evil we mentioned earlier. God does not give us all the answers. He cannot. A god whose actions we can fully understand is no god at all. However, in his death, he demonstrates what the answer cannot be. We do not suffer because God is uncaring or distant or unconcerned. We might levy such a charge against a deity who is only beyond us, but in Jesus, we recognize that God has also suffered beside us. He ordains nothing that he does not also willingly endure.

Some years ago, I found myself reading accounts of soldiers who fought in the First World War. One feature of these soldiers' accounts was their feelings about their superiors. Almost all the soldiers drew a distinction between the generals and other "higher-ups" and the enlisted officers who were giving them their orders. They disliked the generals, viewing them at best with suspicion and often with outright hatred. The enlisted officers, though, were treated with a great deal of respect. After all, those men were beside them in the trenches. When the generals ordered an assault, it was from the safety of a bunker miles behind the lines. When a noncommissioned officer gave the cry "up and over," the soldiers knew he had eaten the same food and huddled in the same trenches. He would be facing the same machine guns and razor wire.

God has entered the trenches. He has eaten the same food and been struck by the same bullets. We might not understand his commands—we might even disagree with them—but we know that he must care because he came as Jesus. The world might seem crazy, but it's the kind of crazy that God willingly endured.

We can come to God as a fellow sufferer who understands. When we experience physical pain or betrayal, when we confront loss or even death, we don't have to describe them to God as foreign experiences. We can tell him how much our experiences suck and hear him respond with that sympathetic "Sure does," textured with layers of meaning born from familiarity.

All this talk of a suffering God is mysterious. Trying to hold the images of God on the throne and God on the cross in our heads at the same time defies our imaginations. Move too far in the direction of a suffering God and we lose a proper sense of his impassible perfection. Go too far in the other direction and we end up failing to do justice to the reality of the Incarnation.

While this tension befuddles us, it is part of what makes Christianity uniquely helpful in life's hard places. Most religions make their deities one thing or the other, either near enough to sympathize with us but impotent to help or so far above us that we have no hope of being understood. Christianity insists that both are true at the same time. God is enthroned above the heavens *and* he has stooped near to us in Jesus Christ. He rules the universe *and* he knows our grief.

Here are some of the things I have said to God in this journey through Elizabeth's cancer:

- "Why are all these people so broken?"
- "Why is life so broken?"
- "Are you even there?"
- "Sometimes I just wish there was some way I could hurt you."
- "I know this smiting thing isn't the norm, but if this person tells me about their herbal healing voodoo one more time . . ."
- "I don't want to deal with this anymore. I am done."

These are not the prayers of a saint. I am not recommending you incorporate them into your daily quiet times. Some of them are probably sinful. However, I say them because I know God understands. He has walked these same pathways in Jesus Christ, and while Jesus handled things better than I do, he also knows the grief from which my honest words are wrought.

There is enormous comfort in this proclamation: Our God knows our sorrows. That truth tempers our vision of God in the heavens, reminding us that he both sits on the throne and bends down to wipe our tears. We can rest in the presence of such a Lord. Even more, that picture of God helps us begin to find hope amid our struggle. After all, God's grief isn't just a picture of compassion—it is also one of redemption.

6

DEATHS AND
RESURRECTIONS

PEOPLE ARE UNRELIABLE, but they die with remarkable con-
sistency. As a pastor, I perform a lot of funerals. Weddings,
too; for years I kept a mental tally of the marrying-to-burying
ratio in my ministry, but given the nature of the world we
inhabit, the funerals inevitably outnumber the nuptials by
something like two to one.

There is a gravity I feel when sitting with the grieving.
A minister's job is not to mouth hollow words and perform
comforting gestures but to enter grief alongside those who
mourn. It is a call to bear witness to this person who has
vanished from the world. We have a deep need to honor the
deceased, to recognize the image of God in their lives and
acknowledge the loss in the hearts of those close to them.

For some reason, I had not anticipated the gut punch the first time I performed a funeral after Elizabeth's diagnosis. It wasn't that I was totally unprepared. I recognized and even explained to her the need to compartmentalize to keep from being overwhelmed. For most of the visitation and service, I succeeded. Then grief leapt out at me, unexpectedly. Standing beside the casket at the committal, I found myself overwhelmed by the enormity and finality of death. My tongue tripped over the familiar words: "Earth to earth, ashes to ashes, dust to dust." A vast pit was opening before me, a gaping emptiness I could not endure.

Grief isn't so much grappling with a thing as with the absence of a thing. It is a battle with nothingness. We barely noticed when the person was there; they were woven into our world. Suddenly they disappear, and we realize the empty gulf in our heart they had occupied. We futilely try to get our hands around the void and force it to be full.

That emptiness is what confronts me in my darkest moments. It is not the thought of Elizabeth's dying that is hard. I have spent my time around death. What I feel is what is lost. Shared daydreams are turned from unlikely to impossible. Casual rhythms that more than a decade of marriage have made habits will lose their context. Jokes will be left without a punch line. The world without the atmosphere of this person I love becomes an alien place. I will be, from the perspective of the most meaningful relationship I have known in life, alone.

There are two mistakes we can make when confronted by such a reality.

One is to downplay it. This is the womb from which false comforts are born, stitched together from half-truths but wielded like knives. "They're in a better place," some say, as if that was what mattered. Of course, the person who is gone is fine now; the problem is, I am not. "You'll get through this," others say, but I wonder what lesser version of me will survive. Besides, "getting through" isn't the done deal people seem to make of it. There are those who vanish into grief and never return.

Perhaps the most dangerous of these half-truths is the promise that God will make things turn out for the best. That is how the biblical idea is summarized by pop theologians; Scripture's words are a bit more complicated, and we'll return to them later. For now, the danger is this: that statement becomes destructive when the good is put forward as if it cancels out the evil. It conveys an economics of consolation. Loss is treated as an acceptable cost because all that matters is ending life in the black. The other day someone said to me, "I know this stuff with Elizabeth is hard, but I just have to tell you, I really think it's made you a stronger person." Something in me snapped, and I told them the truth: "Maybe so, but I'd happily be weaker and not have my wife be killed."

God is working good, but that doesn't make evil less evil. Death and pain and grief and sin are terrible. We should never speak in ways that deny their darkness. Human mortality is not a part of God's good design for the world. Human sorrow is not necessary to creation. As we saw in the story of the Fall, these things are alien invaders. We must never treat them as natives lest we convey a distorted view of the world.

That being said, there is another mistake we can make. The great silence of death can, if left unanswered, leave us in absolute despair. We think that nothing will be good again, nothing bright or beautiful. There is an appropriate sadness we carry in our hearts, but if we aren't careful, that sadness can suck us downward into the slough of despair. While we do not need dismissive comfort, we do need hope. We need an idea of redemption, a belief that beauty can blossom even in these ashes.

What is the difference between true hope and false comfort? In the case of false comfort, the goal is to make sorrow smaller. The Christian hope instead takes it all in and says, "Yes, but as horrific as everything is, there is also resurrection."

Substitutionary Suffering

As we talked about before, because Jesus suffered and died, God can relate to us in our sadness. However, Christ's sacrifice was not simply a work of sympathy but of salvation. It does not just demonstrate God's intimacy with pain; it promises healing.

Jesus' suffering was both *with* us and *for* us. "Surely he has borne our griefs and carried our sorrows," the prophet Isaiah proclaimed (Isaiah 53:4). He goes on to flesh out this theme:

He was pierced for our transgressions;
    he was crushed for our iniquities;
upon him was the chastisement that brought us peace,
    and with his wounds we are healed.
All we like sheep have gone astray;
    we have turned—every one—to his own way;
and the LORD has laid on him
    the iniquity of us all.

ISAIAH 53:5-6

Jesus was not crushed arbitrarily. It was our sin that pierced him. He was broken by us, and he was broken for us. Jesus experienced the consequences of our rebellion on the cross. His substitutionary suffering is what stands behind the insistence that he became "a curse for us" (Galatians 3:13). It is why Jesus speaks of himself as a "ransom" (Mark 10:45; 1 Timothy 2:6) and why in his death, he is dying *for us* (John 11:50-52; 2 Corinthians 5:14). This theme of Christ's sin-bearing death is perhaps most clearly articulated by the words of the apostle Paul: "For our sake he made him to be sin who knew no sin, so that in him we might become the righteousness of God" (2 Corinthians 5:21).

The root of all the brokenness of the world is our sin. We have torn holes in the fabric of creation, and pain and destruction rushed in through the fissures. As the world's destroyers, we are the ones who should justly suffer its ruin. For God to ignore such an act would be to pretend as if the loss and sorrow our sin causes are inconsequential. I have hurt people. I have wrecked the world. Therefore, I should be wrecked in turn. For the death I have brought, I ought to die.

And remember, it is God our Creator whose world we are wrecking. Some clusters of cells in my wife's beautiful body are destroying it, and we address their rebellion through surgical knives and poison and radiation. The cancer cannot protest that it has rights, that we really are overreacting. Some clusters of cells in God's beautiful world are destroying it; we ought not be surprised that the surgeon's knife is poised and ready.

What is remarkable about the biblical story is that we are not simply excised like tumors. The work of Jesus acknowledges the destructiveness of our sin without letting justice consume us. By entering our humanity and dying himself in our place, God pays for the evil of our sins while providing us a way to escape them. The blade of judgment pierces him, and as we find shelter in him, we are therefore spared.

All of this talk of judgment and substitution should sound familiar. I hope it does if you are a Christian; if not, your church has failed to tell you the most essential truths about yourself and God. It is a beautiful proclamation that we should celebrate. He has carried our guilt on his own back. His cross speaks unimaginable love that takes the worst that we have done and faces its consequences on our behalf. That said, this proclamation is sometimes impoverished because we fail to appreciate what it means. Too often we discuss it only in terms of escaping the worst consequences of our sins. Jesus keeps us from burning in hell or being struck down by lightning. While such a salvation beats the alternative, it fails to communicate the true power of this good news.

Restored Relationship

The cross is not simply about rescue but also about restoration. The cross is not primarily about escape from some future punishment but rather about healing our relationship with God. Christ's death brings us back into communion with our Creator: "Christ also suffered once for sins, the righteous for the unrighteous, *that he might bring us to God*" (1 Peter 3:18, emphasis added). This restored relationship means that everything has changed.

When sin broke the world, the first thing broken was our connection with our Creator. That was the rupture from which all other evil flowed. By healing this relationship, Jesus isn't only working some Godward spiritual renewal (although he is doing that) but is also beginning a process that flows out into every aspect of our brokenness. Shattered relationships with others, a scarred planet, and even our own internal shame and crooked hearts can all begin to be addressed because we have been brought back into right relationship with our heavenly Father.

Christ's death calls us into new life: "He himself bore our sins in his body on the tree, that we might die to sin and live to righteousness. By his wounds you have been healed. For you were straying like sheep, but have now returned to the Shepherd and Overseer of your souls" (1 Peter 2:24-25). Notice the three things that all fit together there: Jesus dies a substitutionary death for us ("He himself bore our sins"); we have a new relationship with God (we have "returned to the Shepherd and Overseer of [our] souls"); and therefore we are invited into a new life, one in which we might "live to righteousness." The cross is a symbol of substitution that leads, by way of reconciliation, to transformation of our lives and ultimately of the world.

Or, to put it another way: You cannot separate Crucifixion and Resurrection. The full importance of the empty tomb will have to wait a few more chapters, but we cannot grasp the idea of restoration without speaking of Christ's rising: "Blessed be the God and Father of our Lord Jesus Christ! According to his great mercy, he has caused us to be born again to a living hope through the resurrection of Jesus Christ from the dead" (1 Peter 1:3). Since we have died with Christ, so we now live in him: "We were buried therefore with him by baptism into death, in order that, just as Christ was raised from the dead by the glory of the Father, we too might walk in newness of life" (Romans 6:4).

Sometimes Christians focus on Jesus dying without discussing the reality that he rose again. This failure is part of why we feel puzzled by the Christian calling of obedience. Neglecting resurrection also robs us of one of the essential promises Scripture offers when we consider our own suffering and grief.

Manifesting the Life of Christ

The Bible talks about the death and resurrection of Jesus in ways we aren't accustomed to. We focus on their products— what they do for us. The Bible, while it celebrates what we receive from resurrection, also speaks of participation. We are a part of Christ's suffering; we are a part of his new life. His suffering and resurrection are not just something done for us; they are also something we are invited into.

Paul speaks of our "carrying in the body the death of Jesus" (2 Corinthians 4:10) and his "bear[ing] on [his] body the marks of Jesus" (Galatians 6:17). Peter calls us to "rejoice insofar as you share Christ's sufferings" (1 Peter 4:13). These ideas come from Jesus himself, who pictures his cross as not only an object of our salvation but also a part of our calling: "If anyone would come after me, let him deny himself and take up his cross and follow me. For whoever would save his life will lose it, but whoever loses his life for my sake will find it" (Matthew 16:24-25).

What sort of suffering do these texts have in mind? Certainly, they focus on suffering that occurs because of our commitment to Christ. Peter is addressing people facing religious persecution in his first letter. However, that is not always the case. Paul, writing to the church in Corinth, pictures the "death of Jesus" we are "always carrying" as including all kinds of weakness, including the simple fact of our own mortality (2 Corinthians 4:7-11). Later in that same letter, when he recounts his suffering as an apostle, he includes the full gamut of troubles that show his weakness, not only those resulting from human opposition to the gospel (2 Corinthians 11:23-29). The concern in Scripture seems to be less with a specific category of suffering as with a specific position of the sufferer, that of being "in Christ." When we belong to Jesus, we can view any hardship as sharing in his cross.

Remember what we said earlier about finding our purpose in the glory of God. When pursuing such a God-exalting purpose, even our afflictions become channels for grace and hope. My wife speaks of "stewarding our suffering," treating it as an opportunity, living it out in a way that ministers to others rather than withdrawing from or growing bitter toward them. She's right—and purpose is not the only thing we find in suffering. As we see our suffering joined to Christ's, we also have hope that the life of his resurrection will come into the world through us. Paul tells us that we are "always carrying in the body the death of Jesus, so that the life of Jesus may also be manifested in our bodies" (2 Corinthians 4:10). Think about that. Something in us is dying so that the resurrection of Jesus can blossom in our lives as well. Death, when it dwells in bodies united with Christ, is transformed into life.

The cross and resurrection are the pattern for and the power through which God works in our lives. This is Paul's insistence in Romans 8: "He who did not spare his own Son but gave him up for us all, how will he not also with him graciously give us all things? . . . Christ Jesus is the one who died—more than that, who was raised—who is at the right hand of God, who indeed is interceding for us" (Romans 8:32, 34). We see God's love for us embodied in Christ, who died and rose again. This Jesus is our advocate in heaven. However, this Jesus is also the source of Paul's promise that, despite tribulation and distress, "we are more than conquerors through him who loved us" (Romans 8:37). Despite the way certain self-help gurus abuse it, being "more than conquerors" is not an attitude of positivity. Rather, it is the reality of what we have in Jesus. He conquers death through his dying-and-rising, and that conquest becomes ours, as we belong to him. He is at work in our hardship to bring us through such trials and turn the death contained in them into life.

This same idea lies behind Paul's famous statement earlier in Romans 8 that "we know that for those who love God all things work together for good, for those who are called according to his purpose" (Romans 8:28). Paul is not dismissing our pain. He is not denying the real evil we experience. Neither is he claiming that any individual trial can be simplistically explained as being all right because of some good result. "All things . . . together" are in view; the tapestry of life as a whole is being woven in God's sovereign design. And in that tapestry, Paul promises, God is working ultimate good. Our broken hearts and circumstances, just like Jesus' broken body hanging bloody from that tree, can—through God's mighty power—be raised into something life-giving.

God Works Good

Now, we must remember that in one sense, the work of Jesus is unique. Simply because we participate in it does not mean we are equals with him in it. We suffer because of our sin and because the world is broken, a circumstance we are complicit in. Jesus suffered for our sins, not his own, an innocent God–man submitting himself to the just punishment deserved by his creatures. Likewise, he rose for us in a way that breaks the power of death and sin over our lives. Whatever hope of resurrection we have, both future and in our present lives, is founded on Christ's work. We don't somehow add or earn something in our suffering or the rebirth God works; his grace alone joins us to it.

And yet, mysteriously but truly, the Holy Spirit does join our suffering to the suffering of Jesus in a sanctifying way. Our lives are tangled strands of inert glass and wire, but when God connects them to the power that flows from the cross, they light up like Christmas. The fulcrum of history turns on God's great transforming of a tragedy into a triumph. The Son stood against the powers of darkness and they shattered him, but the very body they destroyed is now seated at the right hand of the Father in heaven. He is praying for us and watching out for us and ruling over all things until he returns. That is Jesus' story, and it becomes ours.

That transformation of crucifixion into resurrection is not some fairy tale meant to minimize our sorrow. Christ's cross and resurrection do not diminish our grief—they magnify our hope. They promise that, as horrible as our circumstances might be, God can still work beauty from them. God is in the business of resurrection. The life God poured into Jesus is still pouring into our hearts. Shoots of green blossom in dead places. Joy bubbles up from the rock of sorrow. Wisdom and hope and peace rise like the dawn, even though a cruel night lies between.

Our tendency is to minimize the darkness. We ignore or excuse the evils of the world. We explain or disguise the evil in our hearts. We tell ourselves that we should cheer up, be happy, as if sheer effort can shift the suffocating blanket of sadness. The Bible's approach does not minimize the darkness; it maximizes the light. In a sense, this light is reserved for the ending of the story, when Christ returns. However, it is already beginning to dawn in the world. God is in the business of working good, and our brokenness is often his raw materials.

This process is usually invisible, but we sometimes catch glimpses of it. I see it in my wife. She has become a beacon of comfort and encouragement for fellow sufferers in this time. She has written scores of letters sharing the comfort and hope of Christ, made dozens of pieces of art to provide a reminder of hope to those she will leave behind, and shared the good news of Jesus with everyone who comes across her path. I see it in our children—there is a softness and compassion for the suffering God has worked in them. My daughter has befriended other grieving little ones. My elder son has a zeal for the gospel that he shares eagerly. The full weight of what God is working through our lives is beyond my view, but I do see slivers of it as if through slats in a wooden fence.

The resurrection of Jesus offers the hope that, even when we don't see it, God is working good. This hope doesn't remove our sadness, but it promises that there is more at work in our lives than disease and destruction. As we join ourselves to Christ, we know that God's promises are true and that the one who raised Jesus from the dead will also work glory even out of the ashes of our grief.

PART IV

God within Us

*S*orrow is like the painful balance of a bleeding wound and a blood transfusion. There is a sucking hole in my chest from which I feel the life slowly leak. It might start to scab over, but each reminder, each fresh trauma tears it open again. I try to bandage and stitch it shut to staunch the flow, but the bleeding never stops.

Yet while I feel like life is dripping away, it never seems to run out. Each evening I collapse, spent, into bed; the next morning, I feel surprised to awaken again. Life keeps leaking in even as it leaks out, and I find the strength to rise, but what I recover never seems to replace what has been lost. I am always running on empty, never making headway and never fully disappearing into myself.

Outsiders think grief is like a broken bone. Set it, keep it immobile for a week or two, and then break off the plaster shell to find nothing left of the fracture except a story and a slight scar. This is not that. Even when you button up your shirt and go about your business, it is with a wince and sallow complexion. The wound rips open at unexpected moments, red blossoms across your chest, and you are laid bare.

How do I run the race when I am so weak? How can I find strength when I am so easily broken? Why do I press forward when the end never seems to get any closer? What does it mean to heal when the cut runs through my very heart?

7

GOD IN OUR MIDST

THROUGH THE HAZE OF YEARS, there are a few things about the night our daughter was born prematurely that I still recall with perfect clarity. I can feel my wife's shaking hand as I clutched it in a crowded operating room and sang hymns to her. I can hear doctors calling out the falling numbers of our baby's heart rate and fiercely debating whether to operate. Especially clear is our girl's feeble cry when she was delivered, a momentous signal that her lungs could at least draw air. There is one more image, though, that also sticks with me: a couple dear friends and a man who understood what it meant to be a pastor greeting me in the hospital waiting room at 2 o'clock in the morning. I hadn't asked them to come. I had no idea they had been waiting. Nonetheless, they understood that pain needs presence.

The night my wife went into surgery to remove the initial tumor from her cancer, I sat in a hospital waiting room between two Christian brothers. Again, I hadn't had to ask them to come; they simply arrived. Their presence in that darkness didn't change our situation, but it had an impact that still draws tears to my eyes as I look back down the corridor of years.

I have taken two lessons from those nights. One is the power of human presence, the need to simply sit with someone and bear witness to the darkness. I remember this when I visit those who are sick or dying. My task is not to police thoughts or to give answers or even to speak at all. What those in acute sorrow need most is another human being beside them, holding their hand, weeping as they weep and listening as they babble.

The deeper lesson is that I need this same kind of presence from God. We have been discussing ideas about God's work in the past, and we will discuss ideas about his work in the future as well. Those ideas matter—having the wrong ideas about God can turn our grief toxic or leave it unanswered— but they are insufficient. If I am to endure the all-too-real present, I need a God who is sitting there in the hospital chair beside me.

Christianity audaciously claims that the same God who rules over the universe and worked salvation on the cross has drawn near to us in this way. God is present with us in our grief. This vision of God is going to be harder to explain than the first two, because I am describing experiential truths. God's presence is an idea you meet with skin on. However, like all our experiences as Christians, that encounter rests on a theological reality we learn about in Scripture: God's presence in the world, particularly his presence through the Holy Spirit.

The Presence of God

From the beginning, the Bible is a story about the presence of God. Even before the first word of creation, we are told that "the Spirit of God was hovering over the face of the waters" (Genesis 1:2). God does not peer down from heaven as he creates; he hovers like a mist over the formless potential of the world. Just a few chapters later, God is walking with Adam and Eve in the garden in the cool of the day.

Sin broke the intimacy of this relationship, but God has been at work ever since to restore it. In the Old Testament, God's presence is caught up with the idea of covenants— God's promises to his people that draw them into relationship with him. From the first calling of Abraham in Genesis 12, covenant is framed not just in terms of promises about the world, like land and offspring, but in the nearness of God: "I will establish my covenant between me and you and your offspring after you throughout their generations for an everlasting covenant, to be God to you and to your offspring after you" (Genesis 17:7). These people are being brought into a new relationship with God, one where he is somehow identified with them.

As the story continues, the promise of nearness grows to include God actually living in the midst of his people: "I will dwell among the people of Israel and will be their God. . . . I am the LORD their God, who brought them out of the land of Egypt that I might dwell among them. I am the LORD their God" (Exodus 29:45-46). Initially, this presence is expressed in the tabernacle, a tent of meeting that was the center of Israel's worship. When it was completed, God's presence miraculously descended: "The cloud covered the tent of meeting, and the glory of the LORD filled the tabernacle" (Exodus 40:34). Eventually, this tabernacle was replaced by the more permanent temple. Again, we read that after it is dedicated, "when the priests came out of the Holy Place, a cloud filled the house of the LORD, so that the priests could not stand to minister because of the cloud, for the glory of the LORD filled the house of the LORD" (1 Kings 8:10-11).

Of course, God did not literally live in the tabernacle or temple. Solomon makes this clear in his prayer of dedication: "Will God indeed dwell on the earth? Behold, heaven and the highest heaven cannot contain you; how much less this house that I have built!" (1 Kings 8:27). God is eternal and infinite; he didn't need the Israelites to erect a shelter to keep the rain off his head. His presence in these places was symbolic of a deeper truth. The descending of God's cloud of glory spoke of his closeness to his people. Solomon pictures this as God's eyes being open to his children, his attention being given to their prayers, and his forgiveness and love being poured out on them as he drew near (1 Kings 8:29-30).

It is worth pausing to appreciate just what this nearness meant to ancient Israelites. In the middle of their camp was a picture of God's presence. Above the roofs of the houses of their friends and fellow citizens, they could see the top of God's house. That closeness was a source of hope and joy for them in their time of need, even as it also stood as a warning against their hard-heartedness and sin. Even in the Old Testament, the Creator drew near to his creatures in love. Unfortunately, that divine presence was limited and short-lived. God's people continued in rebellion against him. This resulted in their exile from the land. Caught up in that event is an image of God's withdrawal; the prophet Ezekiel has a vision in which the glory of the Lord rises and departs from the temple (Ezekiel 10). While God is close to his people through his promises, that is not enough to repair the breach of sin.

As Israel lives in captivity, God begins to promise an even nearer presence than what they had known. Jeremiah refers to this as a "new covenant" God will make with his people. Instead of simply being down the street, he will write his promises on their very hearts: "This is the covenant that I will make with the house of Israel after those days, declares the LORD: I will put my law within them, and I will write it on their hearts. And I will be their God, and they shall be my people" (Jeremiah 31:33). Ezekiel gives a similar promise, speaking of it as the coming of God's Spirit to our inmost being: "I will give you a new heart, and a new spirit I will put within you. And I will remove the heart of stone from your flesh and give you a heart of flesh. And I will put my Spirit within you, and cause you to walk in my statutes and be careful to obey my rules" (Ezekiel 36:26-27). It is with this hope that the Old Testament leaves us to wait for the next move of God toward his people. Of course, the story isn't over. Jesus comes as the fulfillment of this hope. He is Immanuel, which means "God with us." He is the divine power behind creation, given human soul and skin. Jesus goes so far as to say that "whoever has seen me has seen the Father" (John 14:9). Paul calls him the "image of the invisible God" (Colossians 1:15). In Jesus, God literally comes into the midst of humanity as a human being. He physically moves into our camp.

Pause for a minute and feel the momentum of that story. It is not one where human beings fall and then are forced to claw their way back to heaven. We sometimes talk about having a "relationship with God" as if that is something God is simply waiting around for us to do. We act as though he is tapping his foot somewhere up in the sky, wondering if we will get around to him. The cross is viewed like a party invitation from a faraway land; God sure hopes we'll buy our airline tickets to attend.

But the story of Scripture is not of God waiting for us to find him but rather God chasing us down, over and over, continually moving toward us even as we go astray. God wants to be present with us and continually inserts himself

into our history so that we might be drawn into relationship
with him.

The Holy Spirit

As remarkable as that sounds, the work of Jesus still isn't the
fullness of the Bible's promise. Jesus himself sees his incarnation and ministry as only a partial fulfillment of the theme
of God drawing near. He taught that God would send a
"Helper" to the disciples (John 14:15-17). This Helper
is the Holy Spirit, and Jesus saw him as so necessary that
Jesus insisted he must go away so that the Spirit could come
(John 16:7). In the Holy Spirit, Jesus sees the ultimate fulfillment of God's promise to put his truth in his peoples' hearts
(John 16:12-15).

The Holy Spirit is God at his closest but also at his
least obvious. Perhaps this is the reason the Spirit is often
neglected in our thinking. We pray to the Father, and to and
through the Son, but rarely do we address ourselves to this
third person of the Godhead. Yet to understand the Spirit is
to experience a nearness of the divine that is almost incon-
ceivable in its intimacy.

Consider a partial list of the Spirit's activities: He is the
agent of our new birth and works belief in us (John 3:5-8).
In our lives as Christians, the Spirit is a source of divine
power working in us (Ephesians 3:16). Paul speaks of the
Spirit as God's "seal" on our hearts, evoking the image of a
painter putting his signature in the corner of a work to show
his ownership and delight in it (Ephesians 1:13). Because

of this "sealing" work, it is also the Spirit who encourages us that we do indeed belong to God (Romans 8:16). The Spirit, through things like Scripture and prayer, ministers the experience of God's love to us (Romans 5:5).

The Spirit brings God near to us. He also brings us near to God. When we pray, the Spirit prays with us: "The Spirit helps us in our weakness. For we do not know what to pray for as we ought, but the Spirit himself intercedes for us with groanings too deep for words" (Romans 8:26). Much of the internal life of faith is the life of the Spirit. That prick of conscience that brings repentance, that longing for worship that pulls us from the pit of narcissistic self-pity, that shaft of truth that shatters darkness into wonder—these, too, are the Spirit's workings.

At the root, the Holy Spirit is the go-between for us (in our sinful humanity) and God (in his perfect holiness). God is above us as Father, he has gone before us in the Son, and he also directly connects himself to us through his Spirit: "You know him, for he dwells with you and will be in you," Jesus says (John 14:17). The apostle Paul speaks of our bodies as temples of God, an image we should hear echoing with its Old Testament significance (1 Corinthians 6:19). Remember that image of the glory of the Lord descending as a cloud on the tabernacle? If you are a Christian, that is now true of your heart.

All of this is invisible, but that doesn't make it untrue. If we are to take the Lord at his word, the Spirit is an inhabitant of us just as much as we are inhabitants of the world.

The Holy Spirit isn't a religious metaphor but a metaphysical reality. If you are in Christ, then right now, as you read these words, God is in intimate communion with your soul. He is within and around you, interwoven with your spirit and body. Of course, he is also distinct and above you—we need to hold both images together lest we get the wrong idea—but that doesn't diminish his closeness. Through the Spirit, the relationship with God we lost in the garden has, in a real (although incomplete) way, been restored.

Bigness and Nearness

One of the problems we can have in how we picture God is that we place God's bigness and his nearness in opposition to each other. We have a sense that God is great and beyond us, but such a God feels distant. In this perspective, we move like ants on the earth as he surveys us through a telescope lens from up in the sky. We are gnats; he is the divine greyhound on which we scurry.

But God's bigness isn't opposed to his nearness—rather, his greatness is the foundation of his drawing near. God is so great that he can be fully invested in the drama of the dust motes that float in my living room, knowing each of their paths and histories and futures. He is also fully invested in my day with its many struggles and triumphs, and in yours, and in that of everyone who has ever lived. He doesn't watch over us distractedly, the way we watch TV while we're trying to do chores around the house. He is 100 percent engaged in our story, and because he is God, he is also 100 percent engaged everywhere else. He is big up into the heavens but also big down into the tiniest details of our lives.

Even more, God is present through the relational drawing near of the Spirit. The cloud descending on the temple was a sign of God's special relationship with his people. Once we appreciate this fact, it removes the tension between God's greatness and his closeness. He can be both at once because of the work of the Holy Spirit. The Spirit is within us, but he is also above us, existing in and with the Father and Son. God isn't vaguely present everywhere; he is fully, personally present in each place at the same time. He isn't just paying attention to the details of my life; he is actually here. He is present right now with me, and with you, and with my friends in Japan and the squirrels that are sparring in my backyard.

When we think about God, we are considering someone who is intimately near to us. He is closer to us than a friend or lover. The Spirit is in us. We are at the center of God's heart and affection because his heart is big enough that all things can be at its center.

When God Meets Us

I am sitting, exhausted, in my car. Last night, I dreamed Elizabeth was gone. I spent the interminable hours of the nightmare pumping molasses legs through our house trying to find her, searching, yelling, knowing in my gut there would be no reply. I awoke clutching for her warmth, feeling the rise and fall of her chest. It was a dream I realize might soon become reality. There wasn't much sleeping after that.

This morning I sat with a congregant going through their own personal hell. I made the sympathetic noises and tried to say the right things, but the meeting felt like someone repeatedly poking a scabbed wound. It was too close to the turmoil in my own heart. All the insecurities and discouragements of these last years flooded in.

I am sitting in my car, and God is here with me. It's not that I am thinking about him. Certainly, I'm not entertaining lofty reflections about his transcendence and immanence through omnipresence and the Spirit. Nonetheless, I can feel him here, a passenger in this empty automobile. My first reaction is to punch the seat next to me, hoping he'll go away. He doesn't. I feel like an idiot. His cool presence remains, pressing into my heart. I know he is seeing my pain and acknowledging it. I lean my head against the steering wheel and give a few dry sobs, and as the grief pours out of me, it is almost like he is soaking it up, sharing it and bearing it beside me.

The Spirit's presence in that moment doesn't make everything better. I still feel defeated and angry. Yet he does somehow make the moment bearable. Even (in a sense) beautiful, the way there is beauty in a tearful unburdening of the soul to an old friend. I lean back against the headrest and reach over next to me, now grasping for an invisible hand. Weirdly, it feels like I find it, and we sit there until I can manage to put the car in gear and move on to the next thing I don't know if I can handle.

Moments like these are the closest I can come to expressing what it means to live in the presence of God. They aren't events you engineer. There is no five-step plan that forces him to show up. Mostly that is because he is never actually absent. We just miss the quiet nearness. Our struggle in grief, which is just a more pronounced form of our struggle in all of life, is to strip away the things that keep us from being aware of the God who is always here.

Why do we struggle to experience that presence more often? Part of it is simply our own forward momentum. One way of dealing with sorrow is to try to run from it as quickly as possible and never, ever stop. Life is plenty busy just from living in a busy world. However, I suspect that all of us buy into some of that hurry and bustle as a subconscious coping strategy. I certainly do. If I never stop to catch my breath, I think, the sadness will never have a chance to catch me. This strategy is not good—it fails regularly, and even when it works, it's less a place of health than one of soul-withering distraction—but nonetheless I continue to use it.

Probing deeper, this attempt to distract myself comes from a more personal place of doubt. It isn't just a fear of feeling grief that keeps me running but also a fear of feeling nothing at all. Sometimes I don't slow down to experience God's presence because I am afraid he won't show up. This fear is why we need the promises of Scripture that God is near to us. His Holy Spirit is a seal of his closeness indelibly inscribed on our hearts. Even as we are running from our grief, God is running toward us in his love. A big part of experiencing God is simply choosing, despite our fear, to stop and let him meet us. To daily recommit ourselves to recognizing the reality that he is with us, to yell it in the face of our doubts and force ourselves to stop fleeing long enough to grasp that invisible hand and breathe out.

Don't hear in that a promise of some panacea. When we stop, and God meets us, it isn't always as clear as it was for me in that empty car. The dullness of sorrow and the complexity of our hearts means that sometimes we taste God's closeness and other times we merely catch a whiff of a scent of it on a distant breeze.

While I have no interest in selling you some magic hit on a wonder drug of divine intimacy, this is the truth that I have found. Every time I have fallen in exhaustion from my running, every time I have felt like I am at my end, God has met me. His Spirit has spoken the promise of his love. His arms have lifted me, despite my sin and my sorrow. Even when nothing else remains—especially when nothing else remains—he is still there.

8

WRESTLING
AND
RESTING

PSYCHOLOGISTS TALK ABOUT the "stages of grief," and this framework has trickled down into the popular consciousness. First comes denial and disbelief. Next is rage at the loss and the universe in general. After that is bargaining, attempting to somehow turn what is sad untrue. Depression as the inescapable truth sets in. Then, finally, acceptance of a new normal.

While this rubric has some value, those in the middle of grief often find it unhelpful. Not that the categories are wrong—they describe real emotions—but that they are too neat. The labels don't communicate the jumbled agony of the experience. Denial and anger and bargaining and sadness are ever-changing faces of one awful reality rather than events we can pry apart. In a quest to make sorrow comprehensible, we can reduce it to something tidily unrecognizable.

In addition, picturing grief in stages makes healing sound deceptively easy. Once the grieving person has checked the first four boxes, the expectation is that the sadness should be at an end. This is wrong. Grief brooks no easy resolution, and healing is more learning to walk with a limp than ever regaining our former stature.

I live daily life in a sort of confused denial/acceptance until something happens to shatter the equilibrium. Maybe it's some outside reminder of Elizabeth's prognosis; maybe it's just an unexpected diversion in my train of thought. The balance breaks, and I am angry, seething and seeking an object for my frustration. Alongside this anger is a despair at the seeming inevitability of cancer and the uncertainty of the future. While my temperament and theology don't make me prone to grand bargains with God, I certainly make them with my own anxiety. *Maybe we'll get another year*, I tell myself. *Surely, it's at least six months away—no need to dwell there yet.* Somewhere in that jumble, my heart eventually calms, and I return to a place of acceptance, still with a healthy dose of denial mixed in, and now I'm at rest until the thing tomorrow that will set me off again.

The messiness of this process is mirrored by the equally messy spiritual process of walking with God through grief. People seem to expect Christian suffering to be neat and consisting of clear stages. In the evangelicalism I was raised in, the form of every spiritual story naturally gravitates toward that of the conversion narrative. There is a clear before (the darkness, the lostness, the wanton sin), a clear after (the light, the found-ness, the joy of the Lord), and some turning point in the middle, some encounter with Jesus that transforms the one to the other.

There are two problems with applying this conversion narrative structure to grief. One is that even conversion isn't usually that simple. Many of us don't have a clear understanding of the point at which we were saved, just a series of complicated experiences that somehow leave us in relationship to God. (Was it when I was four and prayed a prayer? Thirteen and rededicated my life? Twenty and arrived at a deep appreciation of the gospel for myself? Yesterday, when I realized all over again how little I still understand of Christianity?) There is light before the turning and darkness that lingers after. Jesus is present throughout the whole thing rather than sitting obviously and exclusively in the middle.

The second problem with the conversion narrative is that, while imperfect at describing conversion, it is even worse at explaining something like grief. There is no clear boundary we can cross from sadness into hope, no beach to divide the land from the sea. We are drifting in the ocean, slipping under the water and clawing our way over and over back to air. The struggle is just to stay afloat. Much like the stages of grief, the story of conversion makes us expect people to "get better." In truth, what healing we find is more like an agonizingly slow dawn, months or years that can only be demarcated by slight variations of gray.

The danger in our expected experience of God's presence is that we think God will be present the way Jesus appears in our conversion stories. The Holy Spirit moves, the Father draws near, and magically everything gets resolved. Scripture does not promise such a happily-ever-after fairy tale. Instead, the Bible offers two pictures of what experiencing God's presence is like—a messy duality rather than a list to be mastered.

Wrestling

The biblical figure of Jacob, grandson of Abraham and patriarch of Israel, is not who we would pick as a hero. His brother, Esau, seems more fit for that role, strong and brave and stereotypically masculine. Jacob is a smooth talker, a deceiver, and something of a coward. He comes into the world grasping at Esau's heel. While Esau hunts, Jacob is described as "dwelling in tents," not a compliment in the ancient world (Genesis 25:27). After he swindles his brother out of his birthright and cons his father out of a blessing, the ne'er-do-well flees home.

Years later, Jacob is returning. He has a family and wealth cleverly won in foreign parts, but the impending confrontation with his brother is a rock of fear in his belly. Ever inventive, Jacob arranges a series of bribes to try to win back Esau's favor, but even with those plans in place, he knows the day he crosses the river and the two are united could well end with a blade in his gut. Having sent his family ahead, Jacob is left alone for a cold night with his dread.

Except he isn't as isolated as he thinks: "Jacob was left

alone. And a man wrestled with him until the breaking of the day" (Genesis 32:24). Some have taken this to be a merely spiritual experience, an analogy for the turmoil of Jacob's soul. Certainly, such anxiety can feel like a struggle, but this seems more real than that. Jacob is physically straining against this other being in the darkness. His muscles bulge and ache. However, while he doesn't triumph in this strange battle, Jacob also doesn't surrender. They spend the night wrestling.

We are meant to understand that this is not an even match: "When the man saw that he did not prevail against Jacob, he touched his hip socket, and Jacob's hip was put out of joint as he wrestled with him" (Genesis 32:25). The being Jacob battles can, with a mere touch, tear the bones of his hip from their tendons. Nonetheless, even in the face of such a foe, Jacob holds on.

If you haven't guessed it yet, the "man" Jacob battles is the Living God. He refers to himself as such a few verses later, telling Jacob he has "striven with God" (Genesis 32:28). Already, this story doesn't fit with the comfortable, unchallenging picture of Christianity the conversion narrative offers. This is no buddy Jesus, solving our problems with a slap on the back and a knowing wink. Jacob is terrified because of the consequences of his own bad choices. God meets him as an embodiment of the unknown future, and Jacob does his best to overpower him. That doesn't feel like our picture of piety, but surprisingly, the text treats the struggle with respect.

There is an irony in the battle, of course. While Jacob fights God, he is also in his presence. Many of us wish to experience the privilege of God stepping down from heaven and wrapping his arms around us. Jacob expresses worshipful wonder at the end of the text when he realizes the magnitude of this event: "Jacob called the name of the place Peniel, saying, 'For I have seen God face to face, and yet my life has been delivered'" (Genesis 32:30). To know that God is there, even as we strain and beat against his chest, offers a strange sort of comfort.

As the night draws to a close, the figure finally speaks: "Then he said, 'Let me go, for the day has broken.' But Jacob said, 'I will not let you go unless you bless me'" (Genesis 32:26). What tenacity! Jacob cannot defeat this foe, but even when God offers a truce, Jacob hangs on. He demands not just release but a blessing. It is in this moment that Jacob's name is changed to the more familiar "Israel," which literally means "one who struggled with God." The name of God's people that passes down through the whole Old Testament is a blessing based on wrestling with the divine.

Finally, the battle ends, and Jacob goes to meet Esau. He has contended with the Living God. Jacob comes out of this encounter with two things. One is a blessing; the other a wound. He is now named Israel and will become the father of God's people. Yet Israel is marked in another way: "The sun rose upon him as he passed Penuel, limping because of his hip" (Genesis 32:31). Jacob met God, and the enduring heritage of that meeting is both Jacob's blessing and Jacob's limp.

The Bible is full of saints wrestling with God. Job

complaining; the authors of the Psalms lamenting; the prophets arguing with the divine in the face of judgment; Paul weeping for the brokenness of the church; Jesus in the garden praying, sweating blood—all walk this road in Jacob's wake. Much to the surprise of some Christians, having doubts and fears and struggles in our hearts is not actually a problem. Faith is not an absence of wrestling; if it were, God would not have named his chosen people Israel. Faith is choosing to wrestle *with God*.

The greatest spiritual danger in grief is not our despair or our anger but our surrender. We check out of our friendships, out of our community, out of our lives. Even more tragically, we check out of our walks with God. Such withdrawal is understandable, but it can also destroy our souls. While surrendering is easier, it cuts us off from the very things meant to give us life.

Why do we surrender? In part, it is because we recognize that engaging risks further wounding. Already broken by our circumstances, we feel like we can't endure any more pain. While our spiritual struggles might not result in a visible injury such as Jacob's, wrestling with God can still leave its mark. The only way to experience his presence in our pain is to bring that pain into the open, to acknowledge it and confront it. Such a move will hurt more than simply leaving it hidden, staying on the far side of the stream.

Nevertheless, wrestling is the only way to eventually find blessing. There is a depth, a wisdom, and a peace that can only be found after such long nights of the soul. More than that, engaging in the struggle is the path to encountering God.

I wonder sometimes at the intimacy of wrestling itself. While Jacob in the moment felt the enfolding presence of God as a battle for life, he was throughout it caught up in the embrace of his Lord. His brutal battle with God was an experience of spiritual intimacy most of us cannot imagine.

Resting

We are called to wrestle rather than withdraw. However, if that were our only image, our only experience of God's presence, we would be exhausted. Struggling with God takes strength, and strength is in short supply when sorrow saps the vigor from our bones.

That is why God does not just leave us with wrestling with him as our only option. The Bible also calls us to rest in him. Take Jesus' beautiful words in Matthew 11: "Come to me, all who labor and are heavy laden, and I will give you rest. Take my yoke upon you, and learn from me, for I am gentle and lowly in heart, and you will find rest for your souls. For my yoke is easy, and my burden is light" (Matthew 11:28-30). This imagery is often quoted as a balm to hurting souls, and rightly so. When we pay attention to the details, however, we realize this is no mere banality. This passage is famous—but also puzzling. We would expect Jesus to say, "Come and lay down your burdens and you won't have to carry anything." That is not how he frames it. He calls us to take up his yoke, a wooden beam laid across the neck of an animal so that it can pull a plow or wagon. It is in bearing this yoke that we somehow find our burdens relieved. The rest Jesus offers is not motionlessness but rather a movement of the heart toward himself: "Come to me"; "Learn from me."

What is this restful motion? First, it is a lowering of ourselves. The rest God offers stems from our humility. Consider these beautiful words of David in the Psalms:

> O LORD, my heart is not lifted up;
>   my eyes are not raised too high;
> I do not occupy myself with things
>   too great and too marvelous for me.
> But I have calmed and quieted my soul,
>   like a weaned child with its mother;
>   like a weaned child is my soul within me.
>
> PSALM 131:1-2

In the turmoil that roils my heart, the calmness of a child nestled against its mother's chest seems unimaginable. Notice, though, that this quieting of the soul runs parallel to a humbling of the heart. The psalmist is abandoning his pretensions and acknowledging the transcendent incomprehensibility of God. Indeed, only after a process of weaning—the most traumatic thing most infants have experienced in their short lives—does the quiet come. We kick and caterwaul and are undone, but what we find afterward is comfort and peace for the soul.

Peter pictures a similar process in his first letter and offers some insight into how it works: "Humble yourselves, there-fore, under the mighty hand of God so that at the proper time he may exalt you, casting all your anxieties on him, because he cares for you" (1 Peter 5:6-7). We have the move-ment downward, the submitting to God's control and trust-ing in his wisdom—and Peter seems to equate that act with "casting all your anxieties on him." The quieting of ourselves in humility is the very thing that delivers us from our fears.

These verses are all describing the same experience. When we are brought to the end of ourselves, we are forced to acknowledge our limitedness. Absent sorrow or anxiety, we tend to go about life assuming we can do everything, be anyone, and handle anything. Then tragedy strikes, and this assurance is revealed to be pretense. If we are going to survive those moments, we must start by humbling ourselves, recog-nizing that we are not as strong as we pretend.

In that posture of helplessness, what the heart of faith discovers is that God is near in two ways. One is in his strength. Circumstances that are beyond us are firmly under his control. Enemies that seem unbeatable to us are gnats flitting in the shadow of his mighty hand. If God is with us, then he is present with us in power even when we are weak. Our troubles, while they reveal our weakness, are all within his wisdom and will.

At the same time, as we are brought to the end of our-selves, we are reassured that God is good. That is the emphasis of Jesus: "Take my yoke upon you, and learn from me, *for I am gentle and lowly in heart.*" Peter offers the same reminder:

"casting all your anxieties on him, *because he cares for you.*" It is not simply that God is mighty but that this mighty God is also a loving Father. The union of his control and his character offers the peace of trust. We are falling into his strong arms while also knowing he will catch us and hold us tight.

God's power might be obvious by this point, but how can we be assured of his goodness? The ultimate answer rests on the love God has demonstrated in Jesus: "He who did not spare his own Son but gave him up for us all, how will he not also with him graciously give us all things?" (Romans 8:32). Or, to offer an informal translation: "When the chips were on the table in the cosmic conflict, God was willing to pay blood for you. You don't have to wonder whether God cares. He has already demonstrated his absolute commitment to his love."

As we experience that combination of God's might and mercy, we end up once again with the Holy Spirit. The God who is above us and the God who died for us is also the God within us and beside us in our current struggle. The Spirit testifies to God's sovereignty and his love. As we are humbled, all the unstable things we are tempted to invest our hope in are stripped away. The false sense of security we manufactured by hiding behind our competence or control is torn down. As we fall downward and inward, we realize that the Lord has been there all along.

The more we live into this rest, the more we will find peace amid life's struggles, especially our struggle with grief. While we are rightly distraught over what is being taken from us, the strong and loving presence of God is something we can never lose. It provides a bulwark against the attack of despair and a foundation upon which we can lean and someday even begin to rebuild.

The Movement In Between

There is a tension between these two postures of wrestling and rest. We feel like we can only do one or the other, and in a given moment, perhaps that is true. What I have found, though, is that by being given permission to do both, we find, between them, a way of honestly living out the jumbled emotions of grief.

The call to wrestle is necessary. As scary as the storm of denial, anger, and regret might feel, we need to face those emotions. Guiltily trying to suppress them only stunts us. God's presence with us as a being we can struggle with gives us permission to enter the emotional mess, but it also gives the mess a Godward direction. We are invited to weep and rage and battle with our Father. We hurl those feelings against his immovable nearness. We are called to press into what we are feeling, to stubbornly pour it out before God, and to ask him to somehow work something good.

It is the hardness of wrestling that opens us up to find true rest. We scream our rage at the heavens until we are spent. Only then does the powerful second truth come into play. In the reality of God's presence within and around us, we discover that the silence isn't the muteness of an uncaring cosmos but rather the stillness of unwavering love. We can fall to our knees or curl up on the ground or sag into a chair and allow him to minister to and comfort us. When we are exhausted from our failed struggle to reach up to heaven and move the Almighty, we discover that he is right here with us in unshakable love.

By moving between these two postures, the process of grieving is anointed by God. Sorrow ceases to be something that drives us from him and instead becomes a place where we find him continually present. The lead in our hearts is, by a divine alchemy, transmuted into gold—still heavy, but also valuable and worthwhile. God enfolds our being within his, and all of it becomes a part of what it means to be joined to him.

What I have found, walking through these hard months and years, has been that everything boils down to two choices: I can press into my pain rather than hide from it; and, just as crucial, as I press into my pain, I must also press into my Father.

It came again this morning. Elizabeth received some mixed scan results showing the cancer was growing despite chemotherapy. I was at my office at the church. My first instinct was to retreat from the news, bury myself with work, and avoid the feelings welling in my chest. I forced myself instead to engage, and sat in my chair, head in hands, tears leaking from the corners of my eyes. It was a moment of abject despair.

Then came the subtle promptings of the Holy Spirit: Are you going to bring this to me, or just sit in it yourself? So I brought it. I prayed one of those prayers you don't offer from pulpits, unloading my frustration and fear to the Father. He listened, as he always does. I begged him for a different fate and lashed out in anger, but all of it was in the context of his presence. Eventually the prayers subsided, but his presence didn't leave. I sat in it there, somehow brought to an unspeakable place of rest. He was with me, around me, inside me. Tomorrow might come for us or it might not, but I knew he would never leave.

PART V

God Victorious

Sorrow is the entropy of the grave. It is heavy with the annihilation of good things. It is the memory-eroded face we will never see again. It is the voice whose timbre loses its particularity over unheard years.

Sorrow whispers of the final parting from which all smaller partings borrow their barbs. It is the loss of possibility, of the very physicality of our bodies. It is the plant that stays brown no matter how much I water it. It feels implacable, unavoidable, and absolute. All the fear and rage in my heart come down to this: *The verdict has been cast, and it seems I cannot change it.*

What is there to say, when the last word has been said?

What hope is there, if there is not a Word still to come?

9

THE TRIUMPH OF JESUS

THERE HAS BEEN a strange dissonance between our experience of Elizabeth's cancer and the way people view it from the outside. As much as we feel the sorrow of her prognosis, day-to-day life largely looks the same. There are stretches where we don't think about it at all. Kids need to be fed, dishes washed, and bills paid. Guests need to be entertained and friendships invested in. I still have to write sermons and answer the phone and sit with people in their moments of crisis. Everything is colored by grief, but the basic shapes are still familiar.

Until, that is, someone encroaches to remind us that our story is not as normal as it feels. We run into an acquaintance at the store and they start to cry. An old friend reaches out and tells us they've been following our journey. An offer of charity reminds us of the pitiable nature of our situation. Such intrusions come like a splash of icy water. The story of our lives feels ordinary; it is also a tragedy still unfolding before a watching world.

The story we tell about our life determines how we experience it. We weave the varied moments of each day into a narrative, tracing certain threads while ignoring others. That is why Elizabeth and I don't constantly dwell on the sadness of our circumstances. If we lived in the land of cancer every moment, if we made it the defining feature of our lives, we would lose our ability to function in the normal world. Sometimes people do get trapped in the confines of such a story. That is how grief spirals downward into self-destruction.

The power of story is an unavoidable psychological fact. Struggles with depression, fearfulness, or insecurity are in part a product of dysfunctional narratives. When we mess up, is that an obstacle to be overcome or another example of how we are doomed to always fail? When we are afraid, do we tell ourselves we'll get through this or do we catastrophize, spinning out every uncertainty into the worst imaginable outcome? The biography of our life is written as much in our imaginations as in our circumstances.

If this power of story is true of our internal lives, it is even more true of our lives as Christians. Jesus does not just give us spiritual principles for becoming a better person; he invites us into a new story in himself. We discussed part of this story earlier, in the context of Jesus' resurrection. The life-and-death-and-life-again pattern of Christ's work helps us reimagine our lives and recognize that our pain is not the final word. However, Jesus' resurrection doesn't just shape our personal narratives. Scripture makes the audacious claim that he is realizing a narrative of cosmic redemption in our world.

Our Story of Retreat

For this to make sense, we need to back up and talk about the nature of the Christian story. One of the tragedies of our era is that many Christians operate with a faulty understanding of what Jesus came to do.

When I was a kid, like many young people inside evangelicalism, I was exposed to a certain story about the future. I learned it from movies like *A Thief in the Night*, books like the Left Behind series, and skits meant to scare Sunday-school-aged me into trusting Jesus and not getting barcodes tattooed on my forehead, lest I end up abandoned by my family and worshiping the Beast.

Even as a young person, I felt uncomfortable with the excesses of this movement. It tended to engage in "newspaper exegesis," a Bible in one hand and the *New York Times* in the other, tracing biblical imagery onto current events. Numerological manipulations demonstrated how 666 was the "sign" of the political bogeyman, and while the Bible said we couldn't predict the day and hour of Christ's return, people were pretty sure they had nailed it down to within a year or two. Everyone seemed far more interested in the end times in terms of geopolitics and cars with raptured drivers and potential asteroid strikes than in the actual return of Christ, which was what it was supposed to be about.

However, the problem isn't simply that this approach to the future got carried away in the margins. It's that it fundamentally misunderstands the biblical narrative. When we look at the end of days this way, we expect and hope in the wrong things—and our mistake about the ending then seeps back into how we view every part of our faith and our life in the world.

At heart, many of us have believed a tale of retreat. We are escaping from this world like castaways from a sinking ship. God makes a good world, sin breaks it, and God's response is to rapture away the faithful while his good creation goes down in flames. This world is one of purposeless suffering, a purgatory of perpetual defeat before some happy afterlife spent elsewhere. In such a story, suffering is simply a meaningless reality we must endure before God blows the whole thing to hell. Literally.

That story of defeat and retreat warps the way Christians live. It warps how we view creation. I remember, as a child, seeing a pastor litter, which was deeply offensive to my seven-year-old environmentalist self. When I objected, he just shrugged and said, "Well, it's all gonna burn in the end." Why care about this world? God doesn't. If he's going to throw it into the trash can, why shouldn't we? Living in anticipation of defeat also warps how we view our lives. There is no hope for the present in such a story, only for the future. We hunker down, maybe trying to save a few souls, but mostly just waiting for the end to come.

Perhaps most worryingly, this story convinces us that darkness wins. Sure, we might escape it, but God's salvation is less a Normandy invasion of grace and more a Dunkirk of saving as many people as possible before the devil's tanks arrive. In such a tale, sin is more powerful than God. When his creative power and our destructive tendencies collide, destruction has the final word. God calls the world very good, we wreck it, and the best God can do in response is carry out a faithful few from the rubble.

Too many Christians have embraced the worst sort of fairy tale: "Once a great dragon came. He burned and destroyed the kingdom and left all in cinders. However, a few brave princes and princesses snuck away one night in the twinkling of an eye and lived happily ever after in a new kingdom far away. The end."

Here is the good news: That defeatist story of the future is not the one the Bible tells. And coming to understand Scripture's actual story of the future is one of the most exciting ways I ever realized I was wrong.

Slaying the Dragon

The story of God's battle with evil starts with a dragon. Well, initially he looks like a serpent, since the dragon must appear nonthreatening enough for Adam and Eve to give him a hearing. This serpent stands in for the devil, a mysterious figure who seeks to corrupt God's good world. The serpent offers equality with God to our first parents and they agree, starting the whole destructive cycle of sin. However, in pronouncing his judgment, God doesn't just curse the man and the woman—he curses the serpent as well, promising his final defeat: "I will put enmity between you and the woman, and between your offspring and her offspring; he shall bruise your head, and you shall bruise his heel" (Genesis 3:15). That is only the tiniest first hint of a promise, but it is there: The offspring of the woman (singular) will crush the serpent's head.

This hope for a son that will kill the serpent and break the curse winds throughout the Old Testament. It gets caught up in the hope for a Messiah, a divine king who will finally bring God's rule to the earth. Just listen to the language used to describe him. Isaiah promises a virgin-born embodiment of God's presence on earth: "Behold, the virgin shall conceive and bear a son, and shall call his name Immanuel" (Isaiah 7:14). Micah sees all the world as somehow caught in the pains of labor, waiting for this offspring-savior to appear: "Therefore he shall give them up until the time when she who is in labor has given birth" (Micah 5:3). The seed of the woman is coming.

Jesus is the fulfillment of this promise. Matthew explicitly cites that prophecy from Isaiah in the context of Jesus' birth (Matthew 1:23). Luke ties Mary's pregnancy to this messianic hope: "The Holy Spirit will come upon you, and the power of the Most High will overshadow you; therefore the child to be born will be called holy—the Son of God" (Luke 1:35). This connection with that first promise of a seed of the woman who defeats the devil is why Paul uses phrases like "born of woman" when he talks about Jesus (Galatians 4:4). It isn't the gender of the mother that is remarkable. Instead, Paul is emphasizing that Jesus is the promised offspring of Eve that was to come.

Therefore, the New Testament sees in Jesus the victory of God over the dragon. The author of Hebrews says that Jesus came as a human being and died so "that through death he might destroy the one who has the power of death, that is, the devil" (Hebrews 2:14). Paul uses similarly militant language to describe the cross: "[God] disarmed the rulers and authorities"—the Bible's language for the dark powers behind this present age of sin—"and put them to open shame, by triumphing over them in [Jesus]" (Colossians 2:15).

The book of Revelation is a series of Old Testament images meant to convey the truth about the world viewed from God's perspective. Revelation 12 describes the birth and work of Christ in terms of heavenly warfare. In Jesus' resurrection and ascension, God's armies go out and do battle with the dragon, and the dragon is cast down. Here is how John describes the world we now inhabit: "Now the salvation and the power and the kingdom of our God and the authority of his Christ have come, for the accuser of our brothers has been thrown down, who accuses them day and night before our God" (Revelation 12:10). In Jesus, God has won.

That is how the Bible views the present. The power of darkness has not yet met its final defeat, but in Jesus, it has been definitively broken. Now is the time when Christ is at work in the world, spreading his Kingdom throughout the nations. Here is how Paul describes the present moment: "For [Christ] must reign until he has put all his enemies under his feet. The last enemy to be destroyed is death" (1 Corinthians 15:25-26). Right now, Jesus is defeating every foe, and death itself—that first product of our sin, that root problem in creation—will be the final enemy to be beaten.

That defeat is what happens at the end of the story: not a retreat from this world but the final victory of Jesus over those seeking to harm it. The full realization of the promise of Genesis. "The God of peace will soon crush Satan under your feet," Paul tells the beleaguered church in Rome (Romans 16:20). And to the church in Corinth he says, "Then comes the end, when he delivers the kingdom to God the Father after destroying every rule and every authority and power" (1 Corinthians 15:24). Jesus triumphed in his death on the cross and his resurrection, he is now ruling over the world, and the story ends with his final victory.

Evil is not an unstoppable reality to be fled; it is a foe who will be defeated (Revelation 20:10, 14). Hell was not created for human beings (although those who continue in rebellion until the end get cast there). It is the bottomless pit into which Satan, sin, and human mortality are condemned to forever die.

The dragon in this story, while centrally identified with

the devil, is an image that is meant to include every element of the Fall. As the Accuser, he capitalizes on the guilt and separation from God caused by sin. As the power of darkness, he is the root evil beneath every tyrant and cruel human institution. As the great enemy, he wields death itself, both spiritual and physical, as his weapon of oppression. When Scripture pictures the defeat of the dragon, it means the curse is coming undone. The world is beautiful and broken, but the claim of the Bible is that the brokenness will ultimately be healed. The infection will be burned away. Only the beauty will remain.

The theme of triumph in this story is why the escapist narrative is so problematic. Scripture doesn't talk about Jesus staging a fighting retreat so that some of us might be snatched away. He comes, and he conquers, and he will reign forever and ever, amen. It is not that death wins and we get some celestial consolation prize. No—the first death is consumed in the second, and all that remains is life.

The Overlap of the Ages

In the face of such glorious proclamations, what do we make of the here and now? The triumph of God seems disconnected from my lived experience. It is hard to imagine Jesus on his throne, putting every enemy under his feet, while I'm watching my wife slowly waste away. If death has lost its sting, what is this pain twisting my gut?

The answer rests in what theologians call the "overlap of the ages." The Bible tells its story in terms of two ages.

There is "this age," the world under the power of sin and death. In this age, evil seems to hold all the cards. Disease and death rage. All is not as it should be. Then there is "the age to come," a world where Christ's reign is fully realized. The grave is defeated, evil has been annihilated, and the dragon is cast into the flames.

Which age are we in? In the birth and death and resurrection of Jesus, the age to come arrives. However, it is not until his return that this age comes to an end. We live in a period of transition, a time when both exist at once. The present is like that shaded middle of a Venn diagram, both what was and what will be. Christ's victory has already been won, but it is not yet fully realized. Our age is like the last few skirmishes of a great war. The outcome has been determined, the decisive battles won, but there are still bullets whizzing and enemy soldiers seeking our harm.

This overlap explains the sense of tension we often find when Scripture speaks of the Christian life in this age. Consider Jesus' words to Martha in the face of Lazarus's death: "I am the resurrection and the life. Whoever believes in me, though he die, yet shall he live, and everyone who lives and believes in me shall never die" (John 11:25-26). In Jesus, we have life, and yet we will still die. Nonetheless, even though we die, we will also live and somehow never die. Jesus is illustrating the tension of these two truths. We face death and suffering in this life, but the life of the age to come is also bleeding backward.

How do we live in such an age? As Paul says, "We look not

to the things that are seen but to the things that are unseen. For the things that are seen are transient, but the things that are unseen are eternal" (2 Corinthians 4:18). "Looking on what is eternal" is another way of speaking about the overlap: this perceptible world, and a coming world that has arrived but has not yet become visible to the naked eye. The "unseen things" are here right now. We aren't daydreaming of some pie-in-the-sky future but recognizing what is already real. Jesus has punched holes in the darkness and sin, and we, living in the overlap of the ages, are called to peer at the age to come through the cracks.

Living in the overlap means we don't have to deny the wrongness of the world. My wife spent half of last night puking into a toilet from the medicine that is keeping her alive for a few more years. My daughter asked me who will teach her to do makeup and other "big girl" stuff when Elizabeth is gone. I am lying awake wondering who I'll talk to when this bed has a single occupant. It isn't a failure of Christian piety to name those things as horrific. This age still has a bite.

However, the present age does not define us. Right now, Jesus is on a throne, watching over us and working good in our pain. He is transforming people and offering strength and breathing life into us even as we are dying. This age will come to an end. The age to come will swallow it up, death will be damned to hell, and our lives will continue ever onward and upward into glory.

The second reality does not remove the first, but it

provides a redemptive context for our hurts. The best way I know to express that difference is the Bible's image for the victory of God: Jesus fighting the dragon. Such a war involves much struggle and blood. As we are joined to Christ, we are therefore joined with both his suffering and his victory.

Inhabiting This Story

In J. R. R. Tolkien's novel *The Two Towers*, Sam and Frodo find themselves exhausted from their quest. As they confront the enormity of their task and the hardships both behind and before them, they reflect on what it means to be part of a heroic tale. Frodo recognizes that, in real life, such stories are much harder than they seem. The heroes don't know what is coming on the next page. "You and I, Sam, are still stuck in the worst places of the story, and it is all too likely that some will say at this point: 'Shut the book now, dad; we don't want to read any more.'"

At the same time, Sam realizes that it is within such stories that life is found. Those heroes didn't choose their path; they simply persevered on it: "The brave things in the old tales and songs, Mr. Frodo. . . . I used to think that they were things the wonderful folk of the stories went out and looked for. . . . But that's not the way of it with the tales that really mattered, or the ones that stay in the mind. Folk seem to have been just landed in them, usually—their paths were laid that way, as you put it. But I expect they had lots of chances, like us, of turning back, only they didn't."[1] It was in playing their parts in these greater dramas that their living came to have significance.

Within the story of Jesus, we find the proper shape for the narrative of our lives. Our struggles are not the final act of a tragedy. Our sorrow is not a pit from which we will never escape. Jesus is fighting for the world, and his victory is sure. We know the ending, and that ending transforms our present struggles. They are given meaning and significance and will ultimately give way to the triumph of the Lamb.

To truly appreciate that, though, we need to appreciate the enormity of the victory Scripture promises. With that in mind, let's flip to the final pages and see the true nature of the biblical hope: not souls in retreat but resurrected bodies in a resurrected world.

10

RESURRECTION
AND
RESTORATION

OUR CULTURE IS FULL OF IMAGES of heaven. Precious Moments figurines of cherubic children praying on pillowy clouds. Cartoons of the pearly gates with a bureaucratic Saint Peter waiting to determine whether to grant entrance visas. Images of angel-winged saints with feathered hair and happy, slightly bored smiles. Every month or two, some parishioner asks me if I've encountered the latest near-death narrative of a temporary trip to such a hereafter.

We have been more directly confronted with these images of heaven since Elizabeth's diagnosis. Half the get-well cards we receive have such images. We've been given children's

books for our three little ones full of sunlit celestial pano-
ramas and incorporeal marble halls.

Here are some questions I have been asked about the
hereafter as a pastor:

- "Will we all have to play harps in heaven, or will there
  be other instruments?"
- "Is heaven actually in the sky, or, like, on another
  planet, or what?"
- "When I become an angel, will I have to learn how
  to fly?"

For reasons I honestly cannot fathom, people have
become deeply attached to these ideas. I've always found such
pictures of heaven to be incredibly unappealing. Life in some
stratosphere-realm where my shirts must have slits for wings
and my hair is eternally permed sounds more like hell than
paradise. If the future is a celestial Thomas Kinkade painting,
I think I'd prefer nonexistence. Of course, I can't say that, so
instead I tend to make noncommittal comments about how
nice it is for someone to be in a "better place."

This vision of heaven has no resemblance to what the
Bible describes. The details are entirely fabricated. We definitely do not become angels when we die—angels are the
warriors and messengers of God's heavenly court, a race of
beings older and other than you or me. The same goes for
harps, wings, halos, and Saint Pete at the entrance. None of
that imagery has anything to do with the biblical afterlife.

More worryingly, this view misunderstands the nature of heaven itself. Children's books, when they explain it, tend to tell us that our souls go to heaven when they die and live there forever. That is not true. The place our souls go when we die is not our ultimate destination. It is a layover on the way to our true home.

Some people disparage discussions of what happens after death because they think it detracts from the present. The idea of the afterlife might cause us to make peace with evil in this world, or ignore its real joys, or dismiss suffering by dangling some eternal carrot as a consolation prize. Christians have done all of these things. But these sins result not from thinking too much about life after death but from thinking too little of it. Our wrong understandings of heaven drive those failures.

We cannot separate the Christian story from its ending. This world is not enough for us. Thanks to the overlapping ages in which we live, the present will always be a broken and painful place. But the age to come shouldn't disconnect us from this one. Far from making us so heavenly minded we cease to be any earthly good, Scripture's vision calls us to engage with this world as we await the one to come.

We especially need these truths as we grieve. A refreshingly honest friend once said of their mother's passing, "I know she's in heaven now, but honestly, it feels like she's getting cheated, and so am I." I understand what they meant. The problem with our incorrect view of the afterlife is that it really is a cheat. We aren't getting back anything close to what we feel like we're losing. Fortunately, Scripture offers us a picture that is so much more than many of us have ever dreamed.

The Resurrection of the Body

What most people mean by heaven does exist. When we die, our souls are separated from our bodies and are at home with God. Jesus tells the penitent thief crucified beside him, "Truly, I say to you, today you will be with me in paradise" (Luke 23:43). Stephen, as he is stoned to death for preaching the gospel, has a vision of the celestial throne room and cries out, "Lord Jesus, receive my spirit" (Acts 7:59). The apostle Paul expresses the goodness of this state after death: "Yes, we are of good courage, and we would rather be away from the body and at home with the Lord" (2 Corinthians 5:8).

That said, Scripture is very sparse on details of what this disembodied existence is like. We know that our souls find rest with God upon our death, that they experience some sort of communion with him, and that this state is good.

The deeper issue is that this sense of "being in heaven"—of souls in some other place—is what theologians call the "intermediate state."[1] When we die we go there, but we aren't there forever. The intermediate state seems superior to our current existence insofar as it means an end to our sin and pain, but it is not our final destination. As the Apostles' Creed confesses, we believe in the "resurrection of the body and [then] the life everlasting."

At some point in the future, Jesus will return and our

bodies will be raised from the dead. The Bible is saturated with this hope of resurrection. There are hints of it in the Old Testament: "Those who sleep in the dust of the earth shall awake, some to everlasting life, and some to shame and everlasting contempt" (Daniel 12:2). Jesus speaks of it more clearly: "Everyone who looks on the Son and believes in him should have eternal life, and I will raise him up on the last day" (John 6:40). The New Testament letters stress that resurrection is our ultimate hope: "If the Spirit of him who raised Jesus from the dead dwells in you, he who raised Christ Jesus from the dead will also give life to your mortal bodies through his Spirit who dwells in you" (Romans 8:11); "[We believe,] knowing that he who raised the Lord Jesus will raise us also with Jesus and bring us with you into his presence" (2 Corinthians 4:14).

Paul beautifully discusses the resurrection in 1 Corinthians 15. He reminds us of the symmetry between Jesus' resurrection and ours. To know what our resurrections will look like, we should read the Gospels and see what they say of our Savior's (1 Corinthians 15:12, 20). Our resurrection bodies are somehow different from our current bodies—imperishable and filled with the Spirit—but they are very much still physical bodies that have continuity with the ones we currently inhabit (1 Corinthians 15:50-52). The image Paul uses is of a seed being sown in the ground and bursting forth as a fully grown plant (1 Corinthians 15:35-38). This resurrection, not the intermediate state, defines the final victory of Jesus over death (1 Corinthians 15:54-57). On that day, those who are still alive will likewise be transformed to be like those raised, and all who are in Christ will live with him forever (1 Corinthians 15:51-52).

People have questions about what exactly this resurrection body will be like. Many of the answers remain mysterious. Again, the best guide we have is Jesus himself. On the one hand, his body was different—there were moments his disciples had trouble recognizing him, and he seemed able to come and go through locked doors without difficulty (Luke 24:13-35; John 20:19). How much of this is characteristic of our resurrected bodies and how much is due to the special divinity of Jesus is unclear. At the same time, the New Testament stresses that Jesus was no ghost. He still bore the scars of his crucifixion for Thomas to feel (John 20:24-29). He ate and drank with his disciples, enjoying the physical delights of life (John 21:9-14). While some things seem to change, we will have recognizably human, physical lives.

Without the resurrection of the body, death wins. God didn't just make my wife's soul; he also made her a beautifully physical creature. The way she fits under my arm, the crinkles at the corner of her eyes when she smiles, the particular sound of her voice—those were things over which he said, "Very good." The gifts he gave her in this world, gifts connected with her physicality, are also good. She paints and sews, picks out the perfect gifts for friends, and cooks with an efficiency that nonetheless delights the palate.

If we only had the intermediate state, if we only end up as flitting souls rather than having resurrected bodies, those things will be gone forever when she dies. Death will have forever stolen them away. However, because of the promise of the resurrection, none of that needs to be lost. It might well be transformed, but only in the sense of an already-good thing being made even better.

The Life Everlasting

Even as the resurrection represents a remarkable hope, it is only the beginning. The victory of God doesn't only touch our bodies; it transforms all of creation. The Christian hope is not escape to somewhere else; Scripture shows us that in the resurrection, we will live in this world made new. Jesus comes back to earth, and we will dwell on this earth in the age to come.

The apostle Paul pictures the world as in the contractions of labor: "We know that the whole creation has been groaning together in the pains of childbirth until now" (Romans 8:22). What is being born is a new creation: "The creation was subjected to futility, not willingly, but because of him who subjected it, in hope that the creation itself will be set free from its bondage to corruption and obtain the freedom of the glory of the children of God" (Romans 8:20-21). Paul then links this hope that creation would be freed from its curse to the hope of our resurrection: "And not only the creation, but we ourselves, who have the firstfruits of the Spirit, groan inwardly as we wait eagerly for adoption as sons, the redemption of our bodies" (Romans 8:23).

Our world is broken because we are broken by sin. God is at work restoring us, but that restoration doesn't end with us. Creation will again be the very good thing it was meant to be, and we will be God's image bearers on it, working and stewarding it as he intends.

The way Scripture pictures this restored creation is as a "new heavens and a new earth" (Isaiah 65:17). The prophet Isaiah pictures this renewed creation as a place like this one, but where things work as they were meant to:

> They shall build houses and inhabit them;
>   they shall plant vineyards and eat their fruit.
> They shall not build and another inhabit;
>   they shall not plant and another eat;
> for like the days of a tree shall the days of my people be,
>   and my chosen shall long enjoy the work of their
>   hands.
>
> ISAIAH 65:21-22

The book of Revelation picks up this language to describe the age to come: "Then I saw a new heaven and a new earth, for the first heaven and the first earth had passed away, and the sea was no more" (Revelation 21:1). The new heavens and earth, like our resurrection bodies, will have elements of both transformation and continuity. The world is changed in fundamental ways, becoming imperishable and almost incomprehensible. However, it is still very much this world. God isn't going to nuke our earth and take us to some new planet in a new universe. Like in Noah's flood, the world will be washed clean of evil and impurity (2 Peter 3:5-7). After the flood, Noah walked out onto the same soil he had left, but the effects of human sin had been removed. Dial that up a thousand notches and you've got some sense of what will happen when Jesus returns.

Revelation pictures this new creation as the descent of heaven—the place where God dwells—back to earth:

> I saw the holy city, new Jerusalem, coming down
> out of heaven from God, prepared as a bride adorned
> for her husband. And I heard a loud voice from the
> throne saying, "Behold, the dwelling place of God
> is with man. He will dwell with them, and they will
> be his people, and God himself will be with them
> as their God."
>
> REVELATION 21:2-3

What we see in this promise is the healing of that first break between God and the world he made. God dwells with us on an earth made new, and as we should expect from those first chapters of Genesis, his presence results in everything else being healed as well.

Within this restored creation, there will finally be an end to the sorrows we shoulder in this life: "He will wipe away every tear from their eyes, and death shall be no more, neither shall there be mourning, nor crying, nor pain anymore, for the former things have passed away" (Revelation 21:4). That verse does not say we are wrong to grieve or that it will simply dissipate into uncaring bliss. Our tears are not condemned as a manifestation of sin. Rather, what we discover in God's return is a loving presence that will dry those tears. Our mourning will end because our Father is there to console us and to offer us unending, unbreakable gladness.

We could summarize the difference between this story and the popular error as one of direction. We mistakenly think that the story of Scripture is one only of our going to heaven. There is comfort for us that those we lose, like that thief on the cross, are "with [Jesus] in paradise" (Luke 23:43). But the ultimate hope of the Bible is heaven coming to earth. Jesus comes back to this world, God is present on this world, and this world becomes that paradise where we will forever dwell.

Imagining Eternity

Just take a minute and imagine what all of that means. Contrary to the clouds and harps in our cards and children's stories, the biblical hope of the new heavens and new earth is an embodied, earthy hope. It is about all that is good in this world continuing while all that is evil ends.

That means it promises an in-some-ways familiar world. We will still do the things we have done since Eden. We will eat and drink, hug and laugh. Friendships will continue and be renewed. We will work on the new heavens and earth, just as Adam and Eve worked before the Fall. There will be tree-lined streets and terraced fields, cities and mountains, the smell just after it rains and the salty spray of the ocean. Every single thing that God said "good" to in Genesis 1 will be in glory.

At the same time, such a world will be almost alien, not because it is less real than this one but because it is more. When we picture a ghost or a spirit, we picture something insubstantial, less solid than the environment around it. The new heavens and new earth will be so real, so substantial, that this one will have been ethereal by comparison. If you could take our current bodies and place them in those God-lit streets, we would seem as flickering ghosts.

We cannot really imagine a world without the brokenness of sin. Just think about how human relationships would function in such a place. No one would ever hear a cruel word or feel a judgmental or lustful gaze. There would be no regrets that haunt us and no bad decisions we dread being exposed to. Words like *abuse* and *murder,* *shame* and *addiction* will have no place in our vocabularies except as meaningless reminders of a past so distant as to be practically forgotten. In such a world, you could ask a stranger in the street to watch your kids without a twinge of worry.

Our very experience of humanity will be different. Our labor is cursed in this age, the earth resisting it and making it tiresome. Can you imagine if work never felt frustrating or futile, every minute of it carrying the sense of fulfillment we only taste in the briefest peaks of triumph? What about a world that was our ally instead of our enemy, where things like natural disasters are unthinkable and we view the environment as something to steward rather than use? There will be no poverty on the new heavens and new earth. While perhaps there will be politics, it will be about public service, with none of the double-talk and self-advancement of our age.

The breadth of experiences in this new world will be only more remarkable because we will experience it all in perfect communion with God. He will be there with us, around and within and above us in an intimacy we cannot comprehend. We'll get to experience the goodness of creation in communion with its Creator, and so the joy of it will be multiplied beyond our wildest dreams.

In this life, there are rare moments when we experience nearly unadulterated goodness. A morning early in my marriage to Elizabeth, lying next to her, sunlight shafts coming through the window as I traced the still-unfamiliar cartography of her body. Having an infant child fall asleep against my chest. Sitting with friends around a crackling fire, wine and laughter and mutual delight swelling up to the stars above.

The romantics of our world long to be trapped in such a moment, to have time stand still. That is the wrong picture of eternity, because such an idea is static. In the new creation, we won't feel longing when we experience those moments because the next moment will be different but just as good. We were created for a world more real than this one, and in the new heavens and new earth we will find our discontentment filled.

All the Death that Ever Was . . .

It is hard for me to even write those words in this season, as much as I believe they are true. Trying to imagine a world greater than the peaks of this life seems almost impossible from the valley. However, such a vision of resurrection and restoration is especially necessary for me amid my grief.

That vision validates the loss we are feeling. One of the pernicious effects of a disembodied heaven is that it suggests the grief we feel over dying bodies and a broken world is invalid. That God doesn't really care about such things, and neither should we. "Your wife isn't her body," someone told me in an attempt to be encouraging, but I couldn't hear it without mourning the physical joy wasting away next to me. To say I wasn't in a real sense losing my wife to her cancer is untrue and cruel. God is no more okay with her body dying than I am. The fact that he is coming to renew creation honors our deep sense that it needs renewal. He acknowledges the goodness of that which, when we lose it, leads us to grieve.

If the popular view of heaven denies our grief, the hope of Scripture acknowledges our loss and its magnitude. Yet it offers this heart-expanding response: As dark as life is, the light will be greater still. Scripture does not minimize the sorrow; it maximizes the promise. God's victory and the world's renewal will be so perfect and eternal that it will be worth it in the end.

This is the attitude of the apostle Paul: "I consider that the sufferings of this present time are not worth comparing with the glory that is to be revealed to us" (Romans 8:18). Paul suffered immensely in his life and ministry. However, he insists that if we could truly grasp the glory that comes when creation's labor pains produce new life, we would see that even the blackest moments are fleeting shadows. In God's victory, we find a hope great enough to sustain us.

In his book *Godric*, Frederick Buechner pictures an old saint who lives beside a river. In its waters, he finds this great mystery: "What's lost is nothing to what's found, and all the death that ever was, set next to life, would scarcely fill a cup."[2] I had Elizabeth write those words in her beautiful script and got them tattooed on my back. They represent the promise we need. While I will lose her for a time, and that loss will rend me to my core, at the end of our dying is life beyond our wildest dreams. I will hold her hand again, and we will walk through the streets of the new Jerusalem and the green fields beyond its walls, and all the losses that we grieve will be nothing next to what we find.

PART VI

The Next Step

*S*orrow is like a journey I didn't choose and don't want to travel. I was walking down one path, a familiar path, and then I suddenly woke up to realize the roads diverged and I am no longer where I want to be. Strange shadows loom about me. Sharp rocks cut my feet. None of this is what I intended.

I wish I could stop. Just for a day or two. I wish I could go back to an earlier time when I knew less and my heart felt full. Yet there is no rest until the journey is done, and I suspect that won't be for a very long time. My only choices are to put one weary foot in front of the other or to lay down and die. But *not all is hopeless and dark. Even here, in the valley of death, there is a divine comfort that sustains us. And perhaps, as we take the next step, we can find a bit of wisdom and hope for the journey.*

11

THE QUESTION
OF HEALING

"God is going to heal Elizabeth. I just know it."

So said a woman shortly after my wife's cancer returned. It was well-intentioned and arose out of real affection for our family. Many people have expressed similar sentiments. "God can work miracles." "Cancer isn't stronger than him." This insistence has only intensified as we have sought to be open about our struggles. Some people hear our honesty as resignation. Others perceive it as a lack of faith. Perhaps you've been feeling that in some of these pages. Perhaps you've wondered about it in your own grief.

Certainly, we have asked God for such a miracle. I have

prayed for it almost every day for the last four years. We have invited others to join us in such prayers. The elders of my church have anointed Elizabeth with oil and come before the Father, requesting such a moving of his providence.

God can absolutely answer such prayers. We live in a secular world that finds such ideas hard to believe, and I realize part of peoples' adamant insistence on healing comes from a reaction to that suspicion. Scripture does not share our skepticism about the supernatural. There is no reason to doubt that God can work in such ways. With a single movement of divine power, he could fully and forever remove the tumors from my wife's body. God can move in ways in keeping with his ordering of the world, or he can rearrange the pieces; one is no harder than the other.

God can heal, and he is opposed to the evil and brokenness of the world. He hates Elizabeth's cancer, even though it lies within his sovereign will. We see this in Jesus' ministry of healing. As he makes the lame walk and the blind see, he is declaring war on the effects of sin. His miracles are not magic tricks meant to garner a following; they are signs that God has come to his people and that he is overcoming all that destroys them. When we see Jesus touch the leper and purge him of disease, when he kneels over a child's corpse and reaches down into death to pull her back out, he's making statements about his divine mission.

All of this is true. Yet as much as it is true, we can be tempted to abuse that truth. I once knew a young woman who struggled with a debilitating disease. She ultimately left the faith because she was raised in a Christian tradition that misused such promises of healing. She was told God would certainly heal her if she just believed hard enough, so the problem must rest in her. She was chastised for a lack of faith, or perhaps a hidden sin, a secret evil that God was judging in her illness. This broken girl found in wrongheaded Christian ideas about healing not comfort but deeper hurt, and it drove her away from the very places that should have embraced her and wept with her. Nor is she the only wounded sufferer I have met. There are people struggling with mental illness who have been the object of exorcisms, those with terminal disease abandoned because they raised doubts among "true believers," and far too many saints who have a sense that their frailty must somehow be their fault.

While such stories of abuse should be reason enough to be careful about how we engage the idea of healing, we must also remember the deeper issues in play. Healing causes confusion about our source of biblical hope. It can be toxic to Scripture's actual calling on our lives and lead us to worship things other than Jesus.

Healing in Scripture

One of the basic rules of reading the Bible well is that we need to take all of Scripture together when we consider what it says. Some texts are clarified by others. Many allow a range of interpretations, and we need to make sure our specific take fits with other parts of the Bible. What's more, Christianity often operates in terms of tensions, and we need to uphold both sides of such tensions if we are going to be faithful to God's Word.

What does Scripture say about physical healing? One of the dangers here is that we tend to quote these verses naked, without what surrounds them, so let me try to offer a few categories they fit into based on their context.

First are those passages where God promises what we could call "corporate" healing. These are from the Old Testament, and they focus on restoration from divine judgment. Take the prophet Jeremiah's divine message to Jerusalem: "Behold, I will bring to it health and healing, and I will heal them and reveal to them abundance of prosperity and security" (Jeremiah 33:6). This is not a general promise that God offers health and wealth to all Christians. It comes to Jerusalem as it sits under God's judgment. He announces in the verse before it that "I have hidden my face from this city because of all their evil" (Jeremiah 33:5). The healing God promises is a specific restoration of Israel after he has destroyed them in the exile: "I will restore the fortunes of Judah and the fortunes of Israel, and rebuild them as they were at first" (Jeremiah 33:7). This passage and others like it offer hope that those facing the ruin of sin can experience restoration. That is a sweet hope, encouraging to any of us who have faced the terrible consequences of wrong actions. Thanks to the grace of the gospel, we can be restored. But we should not take these words to mean that physical healing for diseases in general is owed to us by God.

Other passages about healing speak of it with eternity in

view. An example of this is Psalm 34: "Many are the afflictions of the righteous, but the LORD delivers him out of them all" (Psalm 34:19). Notice, this passage assumes the righteous will be afflicted—already a corrective to those who read suffering as a sign of judgment by God. If you read the rest of the psalm, it also becomes clear that the Lord's deliverance in this instance is one that looks forward to the hope of resurrection, not something that necessarily happens in this age. When it comes to the righteous, God "keeps all his bones" (Psalm 34:20). On the day of judgment, they will be redeemed while the wicked are condemned. Scripture guarantees this final healing, but we will not experience it until the Lord's final victory.

Added to these are many passages that focus on the possibility of divine healing. While God might not always heal, the Bible does insist that when healing comes, it is because of God's sovereign power. Take, for example, this statement from Deuteronomy: "See now that I, even I, am he, and there is no god beside me; I kill and I make alive; I wound and I heal; and there is none that can deliver out of my hand" (Deuteronomy 32:39). We should not overreact to a false certainty of healing by being suspicious that it can ever occur. God certainly does heal, though such healing does not necessarily come with lightning bolts and a voice from heaven. Thanks to the Fall, this world is bent toward death. All healing is therefore a work of God's grace. Whether healing comes from our immune system or a surgeon's knife or something the doctors cannot explain, all of it is a part of God's working.

None of these verses promise the certainty of healing that we hear from televangelists and ordained hucksters. No part of Scripture gives some specific, absolute promise that God will heal X problem if we muster Y amount of faith (or send $Z to a certain ministry). Those who want to make the Bible offer this kind of promise must rely on a single verse. In the whole of Scripture, James 5 is the only text that comes close to promising physical healing:

> Is anyone among you sick? Let him call for the elders of the church, and let them pray over him, anointing him with oil in the name of the Lord. And the prayer of faith will save the one who is sick, and the Lord will raise him up. And if he has committed sins, he will be forgiven. Therefore, confess your sins to one another and pray for one another, that you may be healed. The prayer of a righteous person has great power as it is working.
>
> JAMES 5:14-16

"See?" someone might say, "If someone is sick, people pray, and they will be healed. It's a promise of God." Which sounds convincing until we actually start digging into the text.

First, there is a lot of stuff in these verses about the forgiveness of sins. Whatever James is talking about, it seems focused on that particular set of issues, meaning we cannot apply it to every disease and infirmity.

Also, pay attention to the specific promises offered. James

says that the "prayer of faith will save" the person, and that the Lord will "raise him up." Some versions translate that word for "save" as "make them well," which is possible, but it may also have in view the broader biblical idea of salvation from God's judgment. That certainly seems to be what James means a few verses later when he says that "whoever brings back a sinner from his wandering will save his soul from death" (James 5:20). In the same way, "raise him up" might figuratively mean "restore to health"—but it also points toward the resurrection.

Yes, James speaks more clearly of physical healing, but his language is nuanced, not offering direct certainty about the outcome. First, he commands a sick person to go to the elders to be prayed over, and he says the prayer "will save" them. He gives the general command that we should confess our sins and pray for each other, but then he says we do that so we "may be healed." At the risk of sounding too much like I went to seminary, in the underlying Greek, he's moved from a definite statement to one of possibility. There is no question for James that God will forgive our sins and save us. Because of who God is, he also believes in the real possibility of physical healing. But he doesn't speak of it with the same degree of certainty.

Here is the point. You cannot build on James 5 a theology that God will, guaranteed, heal someone's sickness. Those who use it that way are going beyond the text. James does want to stress to us the power of prayer and that we should pray for healing, but he doesn't make it into some mechanism for wish fulfillment. God can work through our prayers to bring such miraculous deliverance, but our prayers do not "work on" God to force him to behave as we might like.

Healing and Hope

As we have faced Elizabeth's diagnosis, different versions of these promises of healing have popped up everywhere. We have been given several books that implicitly or explicitly make such claims. I have talked to people who struggle deeply with the fact that God hasn't healed them yet. Some days, even I feel a nagging doubt in my own heart. *Maybe I'm wrong and some theological error or deficiency of faith or undiscovered sin is preventing her cancer from being removed.* The corrosive influence of such ideas can crush hearts already heavy with sadness. That's why it is crucial to recognize the truth: While Scripture insists that God *can* heal, it never promises that he *will*.

But there is a deeper issue that lies behind these false promises. It has taken Elizabeth and me a long time to recognize it. An inappropriate hope in God's healing isn't just dangerous because it is untrue; it is also dangerous because it can prevent us from finding the real sources of hope that Scripture provides. When healing is where we place our confidence, we can make it our idol.

One of the greatest documents to come out of the Protestant Reformation is the Heidelberg Catechism, a series of questions and answers intended to instruct Christians on the core of their faith. The very first question in this catechism is, "What is your only comfort in life and death?" Here is the answer, a bit long but well worth pondering in full:

> *That I am not my own,*
> *but belong with body and soul,*
> *both in life and in death,*
> *to my faithful Saviour Jesus Christ.*
> *He has fully paid for all my sins*
> *with his precious blood,*
> *and has set me free*
> *from all the power of the devil.*
> *He also preserves me in such a way*
> *that without the will of my heavenly Father*
> *not a hair can fall from my head;*
> *indeed, all things must work together*
> *for my salvation.*
> *Therefore, by his Holy Spirit*
> *he also assures me*
> *of eternal life*
> *and makes me heartily willing and ready*
> *from now on to live for him.*[1]

You will notice that much of what Heidelberg says maps onto the pictures of God we have been exploring in these pages. We see God on the throne, preserving us and working all things for our salvation. God on the cross, suffering for our salvation. God's presence with us in his Holy Spirit. His victory in the hope of eternal life. All these truths provide us with comfort "in life and in death," a phrase that includes every stage of life but especially calls to mind the pain of its end.

None of that comfort is dependent on our circumstances. It does not say that God will fix my current situation, or heal my physical maladies, or give me a prosperous and pleasant life. But that isn't because such hopes are too much for God—it is because they are too small. Our hope rests in God himself. All of his promises are true just as much in our suffering as in our successes. They provide resources for us regardless of our present conditions.

The great danger in seeking healing is that the healing can easily replace God as the object of our hope. He becomes a means to an end, a spiritual treatment regimen we use to get what we really want. By putting our ultimate hope in our circumstances, we have placed it on a shaky foundation. More than that, we are often revealing the ways our hearts are captive to idols. As understandable as it is to desire the end of sorrow or the removal of disease, when we set our ultimate hope on something within this world, of necessity we aren't fixing it on Jesus. We are worshiping a created thing instead of the Creator.

None of that is meant to say that grief is wrong. There is an appropriate affection we should have for the things of this earth. Loved ones, health, and security are all good, and it is appropriate to weep when they are snatched away. However, they will all ultimately be taken from us, if not now, then later. The Lord alone will endure.

Perhaps the best way to think about healing is as a subset

of how C. S. Lewis discusses the idea of hope in general: "Aim at Heaven and you will get earth 'thrown in': aim at earth and you will get neither."[2] Lewis's point is that we can either fix our hope on God or on something else. Hoping in God doesn't mean we don't enjoy good things in this life. God is large enough to include all our desires as creatures, including our desire for healing. We can address our desires to him, and perhaps he will fulfill them in this life, and perhaps he will save the restoration for the age to come. However, when we instead aim at one of those desires, we lose two things at once. We lose God, because we cannot serve two masters (Matthew 6:24). At the same time, we lose the thing we are chasing. Either now or later it will be taken from us, and without God as the foundation, we will be destroyed.

So, hope for healing, and pray for it, but be very careful it doesn't become what you are hoping in. Aim at the Lord and you will find him, and healing besides, whether in this life or in the resurrection. Aim for the healing, though, and you will find yourself in the end with nothing that endures.

Either Way, We'll Be Okay

Those were the thoughts running through my head when the lady I mentioned earlier declared her certainty of healing. Again, I know it came from a place of love. But in that moment, all of what we have been discussing seemed to click into place for me. Things I had always sensed and grasped for words to express suddenly became clear. I responded with what I realized was the truth: "Maybe. Or maybe he won't.

Either way, he is faithful and we're going to be okay." Those words weren't a denial of the pain. They certainly weren't offered from a place of mature enlightenment. I was realizing they were true myself even as I was saying them to her. Yet this is true: Regardless of what tomorrow brings, my hope does not change. The future truly is secure.

My wife is an artist, painting and quilting and creating little pieces of calligraphy to put around our home. Years ago, she made a chalk hanging for our kitchen, a Scripture verse that had been speaking to her. She wrote it before the current shadow of death we are walking under, but it was an almost prophetic recognition of the truth we needed in this season.

The prophet Habakkuk spends the short book that bears his name wrestling with God over the evil and injustice of the world. God does answer, but the answers don't fully remove the pain the prophet faces in the present. Nonetheless, as Habakkuk finds God moving toward him and meeting with him, this is the truth he finally confesses:

> Though the fig tree should not blossom,
>   nor fruit be on the vines,
> the produce of the olive fail
>   and the fields yield no food,
> the flock be cut off from the fold
>   and there be no herd in the stalls,
> yet I will rejoice in the LORD;
>   I will take joy in the God of my salvation.

GOD, the Lord, is my strength;
    he makes my feet like the deer's;
    he makes me tread on my high places.

HABAKKUK 3:17-19

Those are the words I look at every morning at breakfast. They have woven their way into my grief. Even though the fig tree doesn't blossom, even though the healing might not come, God is still my salvation and my strength. There is joy in him even as we are rent by sorrow.

12

WISDOM
FOR THE
WILDERNESS

ANYONE WHO HAS FACED terminal illness has been forced to consider what doctors call "morbidity and mortality." From the outside, everyone focuses on the mortality, the "not dying" part of treatment. However, we must weigh more in this equation than simply not dying. Elizabeth's cancer will eventually kill her, and the more extreme the measures taken to delay it, the more suffering she will experience along the way. Quantity of life is not the only fact that has to be weighed; quality matters too. Finding a balance between these two is a decision without simple answers. We made that choice a few months ago, stopping treatment so Elizabeth could have some normalcy before the end.

I have wondered if the same balance of categories should

be discussed with the grieving. Too often, we treat grief as a binary—either you are in it or you aren't, either you are incapable of functioning or you are fine. It's the reason the question "How are you doing?" is so fraught. Saying that I am okay seems like a denial of the fact that I stood crying in the shower as the water sluiced over me. Yet owning only the despair would conceal the fact that God also lifted my spirits this morning in prayer, or the delight I had last night watching my older son at Tae Kwon Do practice and getting him ice cream afterward.

Grief is unavoidably hard. However, it is still possible to walk through it in ways that are better or worse for our souls. The choices we make about how to move through grief, like the choices we make about quality of life, can make a real difference in how we experience the present.

One of the dangers of discussing "how to grieve" is that people misconstrue it. They are looking for strategies to solve our sadness. This approach is enormously destructive. No one's aching heart can simply be "fixed," and those on the outside should be especially sensitive to how little they understand. However, not talking about these practical considerations is also dangerous. Grief itself can be a destructive force. So while the shadows may linger, we can also lean on a few practical ways to seek as much light as we can in the valley of shadow.

The Means of Grace

My spiritual journey has been enhanced by the wisdom of saints long dead. They often offer wells of insight modern

Christians sometimes miss. One of the ideas in such older works is the "means of grace"—the ways and places where we should expect Jesus to show up. These things don't give saving grace—we have that already if we are in Christ—but they help us believe and experience God's love.

One of those old documents, the Westminster Shorter Catechism, summarizes the idea like this: "The outward and ordinary means whereby Christ communicateth to us the benefits of redemption are his ordinances, especially the Word, sacraments, and prayer; all which are made effectual to the elect for salvation."[1] I realize that is dense, but read it carefully. God has given us "outward and ordinary means" through which we receive the benefits of our salvation. These means are his "ordinances"—the activities we commonly associate with religion. Westminster lists Scripture, the sacraments of baptism and the Lord's Supper, and prayer.

In our everyday lives, we often get confused about the purpose of these activities. We think we do them because they make God happy or because we're earning something from him. We treat them like religious hoops we must jump through to please him. Nothing could be more wrong. We don't do these things for God. Rather, God gave these things to us. They are the spiritual food God provides to nourish and strengthen our souls.

We especially need these means of grace during grief. Our hearts desperately need to taste God's salvation. In the good times we might be able to coast on our latent spirituality, although even then we're probably fooling ourselves. When suffering leaves us cold and isolated, pretenses of independence desert us. We need resources outside of ourselves. At the same time, grief makes it hard to find the energy to use them. Reading Scripture, praying, gathering with the church to receive the sacraments—these activities take effort. It is hard enough to get out of bed in such seasons. How in the world are we supposed to pursue spiritual disciplines?

The tragic irony is that we can easily slip into spiritually destructive cycles. We feel distant from God. Because of this, we don't engage with the tools God gives us to experience his presence. And then we feel even more distant, and even more discouraged from doing the things that bring him near.

Navigating that struggle is tricky because it can easily turn into another snake-oil sales pitch. There will be times when you open the Bible and feel like you get nothing out of it. There will be times when you pray and your words seem to bounce off the ceiling.

But there will also be times when God will burst forth in life-giving power—and we won't have those moments without struggling through the dry ones. More than that, God is shaping us through these activities, even when we don't feel it. Not every spiritual meal is a feast, but the calories we get from even the blandest-tasting session at the table sustain us.

As an evangelical pastor writing to many who are within that tradition, I want to especially recommend the sacraments here. Most evangelicals have at least a vague sense of the value of reading Scripture and prayer, even though we might not be especially diligent in doing either. We feel less comfortable with the Lord's Table. I find this deficiency especially tragic because the Supper is a place where I have come to find God powerfully present. It is a proclamation of God's love and welcome to the saints. It embodies the sacrifice of Jesus, his broken body and spilled blood speaking comfort to us. More than that, it is a place where we get to meet with him. Jesus is our host at the table, the one serving us the meal. He is there with us through the Holy Spirit, just as he was with the first disciples, speaking to them his promises and feeding them in his love.

Perhaps the sweetest thing about the sacraments is their solidness. They are physical seals of promise. Grief can throw our perceptions out of whack. We can struggle to feel like God is near. However, when we drink the wine and eat the bread, God is ministering his love in concrete form. As surely as the elements slide across our tongues and down our throats, so surely has he bled and died to redeem us and hold us.

The sacraments also highlight part of why the church is important amid grief. Again, we sometimes get the wrong idea. We focus on gathered worship either as a duty we are supposed to perform or as an experience we are supposed to enjoy. Both miss the mark. The main purpose of worship is our formation. Biblical worship is centered on and contains all the means of grace we just mentioned. It involves the Word read and preached and soaked up through the lyrics of biblically rich songs, it involves prayers of confession and intercession and praise, and it involves the physical signs and seals of God's love in the waters of baptism and the meal we share.

Now, even as I say all of that, I need to make this clear: We should not turn the means of grace into a further source of guilt. Many Christians carry an enormous amount of shame in these practices. In sorrow, such guilt can be especially discouraging. Instead, let's receive them as an invitation. Don't give up on them. Tenaciously cling to the bread, the wine, baptism, prayer, the Word. God shows up in these places, and we so desperately need to take every opportunity to meet with him.

The Snare of Sin

The devil, Scripture tells us, is like a prowling lion (1 Peter 5:8). Typically we read that as a reference to Satan's strength and ferocity, and that is certainly true. However, lions aren't the creatures we imagine. They spend plenty of time as scavengers, eating the dead carcasses they discover. Even when hunting, they tend to strike at the slowest and weakest of their prey. Perhaps this is why Peter tells us to be on our guard because he is "seeking someone to devour"—the devil is circling the herd, looking for stragglers to pick off.

If the last section is an encouragement, I offer this one as a warning. Grief can make us vulnerable to Satan's attacks. Temptation is at its most dangerous when we are worn out, discouraged, or lonely. Christians don't often dwell on the dangers of walking through grief because our instinct, rightly, is to focus on communicating empathy and understanding. Nonetheless, we need to be careful.

There are all sorts of things we use to medicate our pain.

This impulse is not inherently bad. The means of grace, viewed from a certain angle, are such a coping mechanism. We can find good comfort in this world. The pleasure of a soft bed or a meal with friends or even just the distraction of a good movie can all be life-giving in their proper place. We are embodied creatures, and God gives our bodies experiences and desires that can bless and encourage us. But all worldly coping mechanisms carry dangers as well. Any of them, when indulged wrongly or too much, can end up being destructive, especially when we are wrestling with grief.

Sorrow can open us up to enormous temptation to use things in ways that ultimately imprison us. This danger is most obvious in things like alcohol, painkillers, or pornography. I have watched grieving people slip into addictions from which they feel they cannot escape. However, we can also destructively medicate through subtler sins. Losing oneself in the internet or television, impulsive eating or overspending, or even social isolation can slowly suck the life from our souls.

Such temptations, while they might start off as a way of alleviating our sorrow, can become traps that end up making things worse. This is the cycle of addiction. We start off medicating our wounds from the world, but we sacrifice family and friends and our sense of ourselves to our chosen medicine. Soon the wounds we are treating are caused by the cure rather than the original disease, and we are well and truly stuck. There is no easy upward road out of the valley of sorrow. We may walk it for years to come. However, there is a path downward, deeper into the darkness. In our grief, we need to be on our guard against the ways our flesh and the devil can leverage it to our destruction.

Such coping mechanisms can also crowd out more life-giving alternatives. It is harder to pray or sit in Scripture than it is to wallow or overindulge, but it is also better. I could spend the evening stuffing my face and watching sports, or I could go for a jog and play with my kids. The first option isn't always wrong, but if it is what we consistently choose, we are depriving ourselves of things that offer more joy.

Saying all that makes my heart hurt because I know it isn't easy. When we feel like we are broken, we hear the call to fight on and despair for the strength to do it. If your heart is in that place, as mine often is, let me offer three encouragements.

First, you have the love of God, even when you fail. God's grace covers all our sins. We need that grace so that we don't give up when we fall. God calls us to pursue health because it is good for us, not because he is going to smite us for failing. He is compassionate toward us in our weakness. That compassion doesn't excuse our sin, but it does mean that when we screw up, God is quick to embrace us and forgive us.

At the same time, God's love will give us strength. Paul gives us this promise: "No temptation has overtaken you that is not common to man. God is faithful, and he will not let you be tempted beyond your ability, but with the temptation he will also provide the way of escape, that you may be able to endure it" (1 Corinthians 10:13). As hard as it is to believe, that is true even when we are at our weakest. God will not let us be tempted beyond what we can bear. The main tactic of the devil is to convince us we are already beaten. The discouragement of dark places only enhances this attack. In response, we must remind ourselves that God is present, and he is powerful, and he will support us as we seek to turn from the things that destroy us.

Lastly, one of the greatest weapons God gives us is each other. Shame or guilt makes us hide our struggles with sin. This tendency to hide deprives us of one of the best defenses we have against the devil's attacks. Share your burden with a friend. Talk about your struggles with a pastor or counselor. You are not alone in this, no matter how you feel.

The Fellowship of the Saints

God is near you. God has also given us a community of people in this world to make his presence known to us. Scripture calls this community the church. But the way it's supposed to be, this giving of life and hope and manifesting the love of God to one another—that isn't everyone's experience of church.

Some of this can be our fault. It is easy, in America, to turn the community of faith into a weekly consumable good. We stand in an anonymous crowd, sing some encouraging songs, hear a message, and get on with life. This surface-level approach to the church deprives us of the powerful community it is meant to offer.

Likewise, some of our wrong experiences are the church's fault. Too many churches can miss the fact that they are meant to be a new community living in renewed relationship. Sometimes we miss that relational aspect completely, building spiritual-experience machines or bureaucracies that suck up money to perpetuate their own existence. Other times the relationships themselves breed sin. Churches can foster gossip, factionalism, and selfishness rather than the loving companionship displayed by Jesus.

At its best, though, the church offers a community of fellow Christians who share their lives and their burdens with each other. One of the sweetest things Elizabeth and I have experienced in our grief is the ways God's people have formed a community of love and support. We experience this in terms of practical care. We have been blessed by a constant stream of meals and help with the children. A couple of saints come over every week to clean for Elizabeth. A family of financially blessed believers sent us and our kids to Disneyland. These are all wonderful examples of life together, but they are also just scratching the surface.

At a deeper level, what we have found in the darkness are dear brothers and sisters who provide us with safe space to express our grief. Companions who speak gentle truths when despair threatens to overwhelm us. We've spent late nights with friends who are as close as members of our own family and who love us in a way that makes Jesus more real. People who believe for us when our faith is weak. People who weep when we weep and rejoice when we are glad.

There is a mysterious power in the sharing of sorrow. The foolish feel that an expression of grief must be met by a solution, but the wise know that listening and entering in is more powerful than any offer of practical help. The burden of sadness is made more bearable simply by sharing it with someone else.

I realize you might not share this experience of the church. Maybe you've tried to be a part of a particular church and found that group of people showed little of the love of Jesus. If that is your experience, I am sorry. My heart weeps for you. But don't give up on the community of faith. Keep looking.

Maybe you are in a church but have let your wounds turn you in on yourself. That is understandable, but it is also keeping you from experiencing an important element of healing. Take the first steps to reengage. Call that old friend and have coffee. Invite that couple over. Ask your pastor if you can talk about what you've been going through. Relationships take work, but they are fountains of life.

Maybe you've never really engaged with the church at all. You will have a tougher road. It takes time to build friendships and get to know people, and by not investing in the good times, you will struggle more to find the benefits in the bad. Any church is full of folks already connected in a dozen ways, and while it should not be this way, that sometimes means they won't immediately recognize your needs. That said, do what you can to start the process. Join a small group or other more intimate way to get to know a few fellow believers. Ask someone out to lunch. Most importantly, don't feel like you need to pretend that you're okay. It's all right to talk to someone about what you're going through, even early on, and share that you really need some help.

Lastly, recognize that you and your struggles are a gift to

the church as well. Your experiences have given you a perspective that the community of believers needs. God can work through you to teach people about his love. Indeed, one of the ways people experience the power of Jesus' resurrection is by walking beside you as you struggle to find it in your own death.

PART VII

God in Our Grief

O LORD, *you have searched me and known me!*
You know when I sit down and when I rise up;
  you discern my thoughts from afar.
You search out my path and my lying down
  and are acquainted with all my ways.
Even before a word is on my tongue,
  behold, O LORD, *you know it altogether.*
You hem me in, behind and before,
  and lay your hand upon me.
Such knowledge is too wonderful for me;
  it is high; I cannot attain it.

Where shall I go from your Spirit?
*   Or where shall I flee from your presence?*
If I ascend to heaven, you are there!
*   If I make my bed in Sheol, you are there!*
If I take the wings of the morning
*   and dwell in the uttermost parts of the sea,*
even there your hand shall lead me,
*   and your right hand shall hold me.*
If I say, "Surely the darkness shall cover me,
*   and the light about me be night,"*
even the darkness is not dark to you;
*   the night is bright as the day,*
*   for darkness is as light with you.*

PSALM 139:1-12

13

WALKING
WITH
BOTH LEGS
BROKEN

WE NEVER KNOW *what we're getting ourselves into until we're in over our heads.*

That was what I found myself thinking as I stood in my robes, sweating in the August sun, watching this couple stare into each other's eyes. She had the understated makeup and dress of someone confident in their beauty. He had a crooked grin that revealed he knew how lucky he was. I was looking past them at my wife, still lovely twelve years, three kids, and as many chemo cycles into our marriage.

There was a pause just long enough for me to realize I needed to move on. "These vows you are about to take are to be made in the presence of God, who is judge of all and knows all the secrets of our hearts," I said. "Take them now knowing you are entering into a holy and sacred covenant before him."

Traditional wedding vows are unrelentingly realistic. Perhaps that makes them sound romantic to those who have never felt their cost: "In plenty and in want, in joy and in sorrow, in sickness and in health, as long as we both shall live." I try to warn these young lovers. It sounds so exciting: In hard times, in disease, all the way to death, baby, I'll be there. The unmarried hear in them the enthusiasm of infatuation. It is only years later that they will realize what they have committed to.

When we take such vows, we are naming all the things that will drive us apart: poverty, depression, sickness, and the prospect of our own mortality. In every marriage, at least some of these challenges will arise. We are naming these things not to be poetic but pragmatic. Wait long enough, and suffering will interpose itself between two hearts. We are naming them, and then we are vowing to love each other anyway. To give ourselves to this person, to cherish and pursue them, even though it will leave us feeling more broken than before.

Even in the face of Elizabeth's diagnosis, these promises still apply. My wife is dying, but my calling is to love her anyway. That is what the vows are for. They call me to keep pressing into loving her even though it will only deepen the heartbreak when she is gone. My heart wants to curl inward in these times; the promise I made those years ago demands that I remain open.

Marriage is a microcosm of the broader struggle of suffering. Sadness breaks our legs, yet we must keep walking. I must seek to serve Jesus, to love my family, to care for myself, and to work out my calling in the world. I could withdraw. That is the constant temptation. Yet that is letting the broken part of the world win. My wife is dying, but to let it destroy everything else only makes the darkness deeper.

The question is not *whether* we must move forward; the question is *how*. What are the crutches we can hobble on when both our legs are broken? The fuller picture of God we've explored in these pages gives the resources to continue such living, offering vital perspectives to limping along under the weight of pain.

God's Glory Compels Us

I do not exist for myself.

The thought comes into my head, unbidden. Right now, I really just want to self-medicate. Not anything grandiosely destructive; I want to sit on this couch and watch this stupid television show. My heart is tired from hurting, the kids are finally in bed, and all I want is to drift in the flickering haze of entertainment.

What I don't want to do is pick up the Legos strewn across the floor. I don't want to exercise or work on projects. I definitely don't want to have a conversation with Elizabeth because I can tell she's been struggling, and I know that loving her requires me to enter the struggle. Which, in this moment, sounds about as exciting as getting my toenails pulled out.

I do not exist for myself.

Doing my best to stuff the thought, I engage in a bit of bargaining. *Sure, God, that's true. But I do so much for others. Can't I rest?*

Certainly, he replies. (I'm taking some dramatic license here; I don't have audible conversations with God. I'm not sure how much of this is the Spirit and how much is my own inner monologue, but we'll put it in God's mouth for the sake of convenience.) *Rest is good, but you aren't resting. You are avoiding. Besides, your wife needs you.*

You're one to talk. I need her, too, and you're taking her away. Probably shouldn't have said that; I know it means the gloves are going to come off. Fortunately, the Lord is still gentle in his rebuke.

I made her. You get to enjoy her, but she doesn't belong to you. I gave you to her to take care of. And, while we're mentioning it, I made you too.

Sometimes I wish you hadn't.

Sometimes you forget who you're talking to. Which is the truth. Throughout the conversation, a creeping, holy dread has risen in my heart. I have the sense of an unbelievably huge presence seeping into the room. It presses me against the worn upholstery of the couch. My pity is shrinking in the presence of something infinitely larger. I am swimming in an ocean much deeper than the tragedy of my circumstances. Below me, the shadow of Leviathan moves.

I get off the couch, terrified, humbled, and encouraged all at once, and try to find my wife.

It is difficult to explain how exactly God's greatness moves me this way. When I consider it like a rational observer, it seems as if God's holiness should drive me deeper into despair. Lived experience of it, though, has the opposite effect. Smashing myself against his infinity lifts me and drives me forward.

Having a God beyond us widens the frame of our lives. In moments of sorrow, life feels like one of those scenes in a movie that just keeps zooming in. Houses and trees and recognizable figures and all sense of perspective disappear. A single face fills the frame—hers, and somehow also mine.

Grief becomes destructive when we become trapped in that narrow frame. A young woman told me about the pain of losing her mother. It wasn't just the death that was so painful but also that, along with it, she lost her father too. He became so consumed by sorrow that he couldn't see anything else. He couldn't look at his daughter because her face held hints of his departed bride. His wife's absence loomed so large it filled his whole vision.

This is one of my great fears. I don't want my children to tell such stories to their friends. It is God in his power and majesty who forces me to widen the view. His glory is the hand stuck in front of the camera, obscuring my obsessive focus on the loss. As unpleasant as this interruption feels, it is also a relief. I am brought back to a place of greater perspective where, while I acknowledge that I am deeply wounded, I remember that other, greater things are true as well.

God's Suffering Comforts Us

I am in the large chair in my office at church. The cursor on my word processor blinks away, waiting for me to cleverly exegete some Bible passage until it gives encouragement to weary saints. It is a tapping foot, impatient with my inner turmoil.

Why am I doing this? I ask myself. *What am I doing here?* I feel defeated. Not by some external enemy—I feel defeated by myself. Dogged by this in-my-bones sense that I have failed, that I am in truth only a failure and a fraud. Surely a good pastor—surely a good Christian—would have something to say to help this make sense.

One of the strangest feelings that accompanies grief is the guilt. Partly, it is born of lowered capacities. My energy levels are less than they were before the cancer. My focus is divided, a distracting static in the back of my mind, keeping me from fully engaging. Even writing these words takes an effort of will I didn't use to feel.

Layered on the guilt of my weakness is that of real failures. There are nights where I don't get off the couch. My patience with our kids is paper-thin. Sometimes anger at Elizabeth's diagnosis leaves me feeling angry at her. While sins borne out of grief warrant sympathy, they are still sins, and people are still hurt by them.

And, too, I have this broader, almost existential sense that somehow, I am to blame. I can't really explain it. Intellectually, I know that none of this is my fault, but I can't escape the persistent thought that maybe it is. Are we being punished for something? Is there some unknown choice that caused Elizabeth's sickness? What if we had only found it earlier?

Under these layers of guilt, I'm left discouraged and turn inward. The more I do, the guiltier I feel. The viciously circular symmetry of these feelings threatens to drag me ever deeper into defeat.

During these cycles of self-hatred, I am drawn back to the cross. God suffers beside and before me. As I slump over my desk, the vision that rises in my mind's eye is of Jesus, battered and impaled. Our brutalized Lord speaks peace to my conscience in two ways.

First, he dignifies my struggle. The pain I feel is an opportunity to join myself to Christ. In the cross, Jesus' suffering provides a story within which mine can be redefined. Jesus was weak under the burden of his cross—in perhaps the most beautiful moment of the crucifixion, he wasn't even able to carry the instrument of his execution on his own back (Matthew 27:32). My weakness makes me more like him, not less. What's more, Jesus is an incarnate testimony to the fact that our suffering is not a measure of our deserving, at least not in a one-for-one way. While pain as a whole is a result of human sin, I cannot draw simple lines from this pain to that particular sin. If God himself suffered unjustly, we shouldn't assume that hardship is a sign of his disfavor.

The cross also speaks comfort to my warranted guilt. In my grief, I have sinned. I allow it to cause me to strike out at others and fail to pursue God's glory. The deepest wonder of the cross is that Jesus didn't just suffer alongside me in sympathy or before me as an example. He suffered *for* me, paying for these sins, erecting a sanctuary of grace where my heart can find shelter. The factor that determines my standing with God is neither my circumstances nor how I respond to my circumstances. It is the blood of Jesus. God is delighted in me because he views me through the lens of his Son. He does not see me as I am, a broken and remorseful man in a swivel chair unable to compose his thoughts. God sees me the way he sees Jesus, as his true child: with love and pleasure in his eyes.

God's Presence Sustains Us

Prayer has never been particularly easy for me. I can write and extemporize eloquent-enough prayers for the public parts of my ministry. They sound heartfelt, a careful balance of personal authenticity and theological insight. However, when I pray in private, it is often a stammering affair of half-finished sentences and wandering thoughts.

That deficiency is front and center this morning. I'm bent on an old kneeling rail a friend found me at an antique shop. Last night, I had another one of the nightmares where Elizabeth was gone, and while I'm drinking coffee fast enough to burn my tongue, I can't wash the taste of fear from my mouth. I am trying to cover the daily requests for our family and church I know I'm supposed to bring before God's throne. Instead, my mind keeps wandering to questions about the future. How will I take care of our kids as a single father? Will I be able to continue in ministry? Will I be able to continue as a human being?

The tendency of my heart in the face of such worries is to stop talking with God about my fears and instead to try to overcome them by my own ingenuity. This tendency lies behind my wayward mind. A book I once read suggested dealing with wandering thoughts in prayer by following them and lifting up whatever your distractions are as a part of your intercession. Today, as I try to do that, chasing my anxieties and frustrations, all I feel is angry.

You did this to me, I think. *How can I also look to you to get me through it?*

The outburst takes me aback. Clearly there are some messy things happening in my heart. I wait for the rebuke, but it doesn't come. Instead, as I sit speechless, the silence settles over my shoulders like a blanket. It isn't the hollow silence of death but the wordless presence of a Father. My fingers trace the grain of the stained wood. My heartbeat slows. I am here, and God is with me, and I rest in that space until a cramp in my knees tells me it's time to return to the list of intercessions.

I wouldn't say the prayers flow easily, but at least they come.

When Jacob wrestled with God, the blessing only came because he held on like a dog with a bone. The same is true of experiencing the presence of God in my grief. There are moments that I feel it, but they are hard-won, usually on the far side of spiritual struggle. Of course, God is with me. The

Spirit indwells me. The Son intercedes for me. The Father watches over my steps and has numbered the hairs on my head. However, I can't sidestep the struggle. God's presence is a reality I know but that I must fight to experience. I must keep clawing upward, even when he feels absent to my heart.

At the same time, on the far end of that struggle, I discover that what I believe is indeed true. He has been there all along. Seeking God is a perpetual discovering that he is not far from us. We look all over the universe for him, only to at last stub our toes and, looking down, discover he is right here.

God's Victory Redefines Us

It is nighttime, and while my wife sings to the boys in their room, I lay with my daughter and talk. It is our tradition— we look at each other in her bed and she asks me about a list of topics as varied as her youthful enthusiasm. Some evenings cover electricity or astronomy or theology, but tonight she wants to talk about cancer.

My children have many questions about death. We didn't force the implications of Elizabeth's prognosis on them right away. It is important to give kids space until they are ready to meet such terrible ideas on their own terms. When the questions came, though, we also didn't lie to them. The day our oldest two gave voice to it—"Will Mommy die from the cancer?"—we told them, "Yes, she probably will. Not right now, it will probably be a couple of years, but it will kill her."

My kids' questions are divided into two categories. There are the practical ones: "Will she die at home? What will it feel like? Who will take care of us?" For these questions, the specifics don't matter—concrete little minds cannot wrap around the abstract enormity of the future. Mostly, they just want to know that such answers exist, that the adults in their lives have a plan.

Tonight, though, is going to involve the second set of questions, those about what comes after death. Suspicious as I am of disembodied tales about heaven, we always focus on the new heavens and new earth. As a result, the questions often grow out of experiences of this age. What will it look like? (Like this world, but better somehow.) Will there be mosquitoes there? (Probably, but we'll understand what they're for.) Ice cream? (Definitely.) Will people have children? (I don't really want to get into the theological or physiological details of that with an eight-year-old.) Will we explore other planets? (I think so, although the Bible doesn't say.)

I regard these as important questions, and I always do my best to answer them with as much clarity and honesty as possible. That often means I say, "I'm not sure." It is wonderful to watch my daughter process our future hope. In her childlike faith, she grasps something that many adults miss. We live in a world of life, and while there is death in the middle, there is never-ending life again on the far side.

Now that the interrogation is over, my daughter ponders the answers and then rests her head against my chest. "I'm going to miss her," she says.

"So will I," I reply.

"I'm going to write down all the things we do so I can

read it to her after the resurrection," she says, and then looks confused when I press her against me so she doesn't see the tears welling in my eyes.

God wins at the end of this thing. I say that over and over, every day. Cancer does not have the last word. Death does not have the last word. Satan does not have the last word. Our broken bodies will be restored, our disfigured world will be renewed, and this brief moment, full of joy and agony, is only the first half bite of a feast that will never end.

People talk about the afterlife as a consolation prize. It is the opiate of the masses. It is the trading of what we truly desire—peace on earth and happiness in creation—for retreat into the realm of ghosts. Perhaps that is true of the folktales people mistake for Christianity, but not of the full-orbed hope of Scripture. Resurrection is essential to truly live. If this fleeting moment together is all that we have, if this woman I love ends up food for worms and her graceful presence is forever stolen from the world, then get me a bottle of whiskey and leave me to despair. The only way we endure death in such a world is by burying our heads in the dirt until it opens and covers us for the last time.

That is not the story of this world. God wins at the end of this thing. It is what motivates me to love and work in the present, knowing that everything done for the Lord will endure. It is what lets me look death in the face and not be undone, knowing it is a beaten foe. Jesus Christ, still God in human flesh, will return to this world, my wife's scarred body will rise restored, and I will look into her smiling eyes with their crinkling corners once more and I will tell her, "I've missed you," and then we will go out into an earth where no one will miss anyone ever again and God shines over it all like the sun. That is the story that enables me to live.

I grew up in a family of musicians and have done my fair share of songwriting over the years. Elizabeth jokingly said I should write her a song for her funeral, so I did. I don't know that we'll use it—there are too many good hymns she loves—but here it is:

Darling, we'll meet again
When the broken are welcomed in
Where the widow and orphan
Find family and friends
Oh darling, we'll meet again.
At the death of all longing and aching
He will dry every tear by his hand
And the finding will swallow the taking
Oh darling, I'll see you then.

Darling, we'll meet again
When our Father calls us children
And our spirits get flesh and the Son descends
Oh darling, we'll meet again.
Our sorrows may last for the evening
But night turns to light in the end
And this is the comfort that keeps me
Oh darling, I'll see you then.

Darling, we'll meet again
At the wedding of earth and heaven
And we'll walk through the golden Jerusalem
Oh darling, we'll meet again.
On the terrace-lined hills of the righteous
We'll be free from the burden of sin
And we'll laugh at the grave that could never undo us
For Jesus who died and who rose has renewed us
And the glory and goodness of God will shine through us
Oh darling, I'll see you then.

God in Our Grief

Such is the fabric of my days. I don't know whether those moments feel familiar to you. Everyone's experience of suffering is unique, and I don't presume to speak for anyone but myself. My hope, though, is that you find in the tapestry of God's character the threads to support you through your pain.

The other day, Elizabeth commented to me that she struggles with how people look at her postcancer. They think that the diagnosis must be the end of everything good in her world. As life-shattering as such an event has been, there is also what she called a "strange blessedness" in this valley. I know of no better way to express it than the words she used:

I have discovered things in this season I have never
really known before. God has shown up, the way
I always believed he would but was never sure.
His promises are true. He will carry us. He does

comfort us. Those realities have become more real for me as I'm dying than they ever were before. I don't think I could have known them this way without the cancer and the sadness it brings.

Don't hear in that a denial of the suffering. She is heavy with it; we both are. The process of becoming more like Jesus often requires us to be torn to pieces before we can be stitched back together into something new. God is good, but grief is hard.

Part of me would gladly trade whatever intimacy with God we've discovered for a life where we could grow old together. Yet she is right. The fires of affliction do produce a refined sense of the nearness of our Father.

Epilogue

I'M WRITING THESE WORDS from further down the road. The book you read was written on the journey toward my wife's passing; I thought it appropriate to end with a few words from the far side.

Elizabeth died on All Hallows' Eve, the day before the church remembers those saints who have gone before us. She went after several merciless weeks during which we cared for her and watched her fade. I called our children into the room as she choked out her final breaths. We sang hymns to her; she left us in the middle of "It Is Well with My Soul." I watched her body cease to live, her lips turn blue, the way she shrank in on herself and was no more. We wept from our guts, and I kissed her forehead and pronounced the benediction over her lifeless form.

Elizabeth is resting with her Father now. She has passed through the Jordan, and we cannot glimpse her there on Canaan's shore. Despite years of knowing it was coming, despite months of hearing its footsteps approaching in the hall, death still arrives as a surprise. You aren't ready for it. It always comes too soon. There are still a hundred questions unasked and stories unshared.

Some days I feel like I'm living in a bombed-out house, going through the motions of domestic life while trying to ignore the rubble and gaping holes all around me. There is a perpetual itch at the back of my mind, a longing to just see her, just talk to her, once more. Every time our kids say something unexpected or handle a situation with an aplomb that reveals their maturing, I instinctively want to catch her eye. Every project around the house that I complete, I want to show her, to communicate love by serving her, only to realize there is no longer someone there for me to serve. I keep almost saying "we" and then catching myself, amending it to the first-person singular. Her absence is a pressure that is sometimes excruciating and never fully gone.

And yet, for all of that, God is still reigning over me, still going before me, still dwelling in me and winning the victory I could never win.

Christianity does not offer us an end to our suffering in this life. That is a great danger in how people come to books about grief—a danger I've tried to warn against in these pages. We want the pain to end, and we are not interested in anything that lacks such anesthetic aims. Every two-bit god of this world offers us such an escape; the Lord offers something greater.

Growing in your sense of God's greatness and nearness will not repair the hole in your chest. Elizabeth made me a photo book of our story, and as I read it to our kids last night, I shook with sobs and could barely finish. I desperately miss her, and things will continue to be very hard and very painful for a very long time. Even when years have passed and we have built new lives, the scars will remain. I think sometimes of Job of Uz after the storm and his humbling vindication.

God gives him new flocks and herds and sons and daughters, yet how his heart must have ached as he watched those children frolic in the meadow, intermingled with the phantoms of past children forever absent.

Suffering is unavoidably hard. However, I continue to find that suffering in the presence of God offers two things no worldly hope can match.

One is that it makes grief confrontable. If we must stand alone facing the silent enormity of death, we must either turn away in denial or collapse in utter despair. It is too big for us to look on it honestly, to admit what it does to those we love and what it will, in the end, do to us. And yet it must be confronted, or else it will diminish us. If we never arrive at a place where we can name what we have lost and will lose, we will move through life as half people, lessened from hiding huge swaths of our souls.

God, in his greatness and kindness and presentness, is an anchor which holds us fast against the torrent of grief. We can let pain wash over us, and though we will emerge battered, we will not be swept out to be lost at sea. God is an enormity that speaks life and purpose to us far greater and more deeply than death can speak despair. So we are able to look it in the teeth and name it for what it is and what it has done to us. Truly walking with God makes our sorrow nameable, as the Psalms exemplify over and over. We don't have to hide from it if we are hidden in him.

Suffering in the presence of God also provides a sense of purpose that allows us to continue living even as we grieve.

Losing Elizabeth has forced me to confront the fact that some significant part of what got me up in the morning and made me a decent human being was a desire to live for her. Not all of that is bad, and I think some people would even view it as noble, but even something as compelling as love for a spouse is not a sufficient motivation to truly flourish. After all, Elizabeth is dead, and what is there to get me out of bed now?

A life lived with God is of necessity also a life lived for God. The more we comprehend his sacrificial death, experience his indwelling presence, and anticipate his eternal hope, the more his purposes become our driving delight. We seek to live for him not out of duty or peer pressure or worldly benefits or any of the other trappings of religion, but simply because his pleasure is enough.

Such a transformation is only ever incomplete in this life, and it has only partially been realized in my heart. However, even my imperfect experience has taught me this: We can endure all things if our purpose is to live for God. It is an aspiration both great enough and indestructible enough that even death cannot strip it away, and it is offered with the sustaining grace that will support us even as we stumble in its pursuit. Yet the only way to find such a purpose is to press into the one who provides it rather than sinking into ourselves.

I am here, and God is here, and so I continue to live and hope and love and battle, even as I also weep and ache. That is the journey. It is a hard road, but it is walkable because he walks with us and before us, because he reigns over us, and because he dwells on its far side.

Acknowledgments

I AM TERRIBLE AT THANKING PEOPLE, not because I'm not grateful but because I don't know where to start and stop. A book like this is a product of many peoples' input, and the author even more so. That said, there are several people I want to express gratitude to for shaping me and this book.

My parents, who gave me a love of books and of Jesus.

KJ, Jake, Micah, Gray, and the rest of the gang, for years spent arguing with me until I wasn't a total idiot. In a world where some men struggle to find friendships, you brothers continue to shape and mold me into a (mostly) better human being.

The pastors who taught me what it means to be a shepherd and a student of God, especially Andrew Petro, Mike Hsu, and Mark Ryan.

Connie McGhee, Crystal Davy, Gary Miles, Lori Taylor, and Rebecca Tredway for reading parts of this thing and helping to shape its final form.

Kishwaukee EPC, for being such a joy to pastor and for giving me the space to write.

Don Gates, for taking a long shot.

Don Pape and everyone else at NavPress for all the help—especially Caitlyn Carlson and Elizabeth Schroll, who, like all good editors, worked the alchemy of turning my base elements into gold.

Most of all, I'm grateful to you, Elizabeth. You aren't around to read this, but you were a better partner than I ever deserved. May your eyes be ever crinkled with laughter and your heart be ever full of love.

Notes

INTRODUCTION

1. Arthur Bennett, ed., *The Valley of Vision: A Collection of Puritan Prayers and Devotions* (Edinburgh: Banner of Truth Trust, 2002), xxv.

1: CONFRONTING SUFFERING

1. C. S. Lewis, *The Four Loves* (New York: Harcourt Brace Jovanovich, 1991), 121.
2. John Bunyan, *Pilgrim's Progress: From This World to That Which Is to Come* (Uhrichsville, OH: Barbour, 1989), 120.

3: HE SITS ENTHRONED

1. According to the National Oceanic and Atmospheric Administration, "Oceans & Coasts," accessed August 3, 2020, https://www.noaa.gov /oceans-coasts.

9: THE TRIUMPH OF JESUS

1. J. R. R. Tolkien, *The Two Towers* (New York: Houghton Mifflin, 1954), 320–21.

10: RESURRECTION AND RESTORATION

1. If this is a new idea to you, here are a few places for further reading: Randy Alcorn, *Heaven* (Carol Stream, IL: Tyndale, 2011), 41–76; Anthony A. Hoekema, *The Bible and the Future* (Grand Rapids, MI: Eerdmans, 1979) 92–108; Wayne Grudem, *Systematic Theology: An Introduction to Biblical Doctrine* (Grand Rapids, MI: Zondervan, 1994), 816–24.
2. Frederick Buechner, *Godric* (San Francisco: HarperSanFrancisco, 1983), 96.

11: THE QUESTION OF HEALING

1. "The Heidelberg Catechism," Canadian Reformed Theological Seminary, accessed August 3, 2020, http://www.heidelberg-catechism.com/en /lords-days/1.html.
2. C. S. Lewis, *Mere Christianity* (New York: HarperCollins, 2001), 134.

12: WISDOM FOR THE WILDERNESS

1. Westminster Shorter Catechism, pcaac.org, 88, accessed July 21, 2020, https://www.pcaac.org/wp-content/uploads/2019/11/ShorterCatechism withScriptureProofs.pdf.